The Garland Library of War and Peace

The Garland Library of War and Peace

Under the General Editorship of
Blanche Wiesen Cook, *John Jay College, C.U.N.Y.*
Sandi E. Cooper, *Richmond College, C.U.N.Y.*
Charles Chatfield, *Wittenberg University*

Peace with Honour

An Enquiry into the War Convention

by

A. A. Milne

with a new introduction
for the Garland Edition by
Sylvia Strauss

Garland Publishing, Inc., New York & London
1972

The new introduction for this
Garland Library Edition is Copyright © 1972, by
Garland Publishing Inc.

All Rights Reserved

Library of Congress Cataloging in Publication Data

Milne, Alan Alexander, 1882-1956.
    Peace with honour.

    Reprint of the 1934 ed., issued in series: The
Garland library of war and peace.
    1. War. 2. Peace. I. Title. II. Series: The
Garland library of war and peace.
JX1953.M66 1972   327'.172   70-148380
ISBN 0-8240-0475-2

Printed in the United States of America

Introduction

Perhaps a book as idealistic in intent and ingenuous in outlook as Peace with Honour can only be understood in the context of the trauma induced by World War I.

The prewar peace movement was not powerful enough to prevent England's entry into the war. When Belgium was invaded, Sir Edward Grey, British foreign secretary, settled the issue by insisting that England could not stand aside without sacrificing her "respect" and "good name" and "reputation." He keynoted the almost casual manner of entry by his assertion that "if we are engaged in war, we shall suffer but little more than we shall suffer if we stand aside."

The implied optimism was hardly justified by events. The war failed to end with the expected dispatch and developed into a frustrating stalemate. If the peace movement was virtually impotent before the war, it began to revive and burgeon as the catastrophe that was World War I began to unfold. The Union of Democratic Control was formed by E.D. Morel in 1914. It sought to answer why the war had occurred in the first place and found it in the secret negotiations and diplomatic miscalculations that had characterized the prewar period. Determined

INTRODUCTION

that such errors must not be allowed to happen again, opponents of the war like J.A. Hobson and Lowes Dickinson proposed an international organization to arbitrate future disputes in an open forum. As a prerequisite for a viable organization, they generally advocated a compromise negotiated peace on the theory, widely publicized before the war, that no one could actually win a war in the twentieth century, and on the assumption that all nations were equally culpable in inciting the world to war.

The war did not end before ten million people were dead and frustration had turned to bitterness. To justify the casualties, a wide spectrum of the peoples who had been directly engaged wanted to believe that the war had indeed been a war to end war, and the League of Nations was much touted as the hope of the world for future peace. This hope proved unfounded as the various powers refused to surrender enough of their sovereignty to give the organization force. When the United States refused to join, it became little more than an international debating society. Nations which refused to conform to its decisions simply walked out. Both Japan and Germany used this device to test the League's effectiveness and neither was called to account.

The failure of the League by the early 1930s coincided with a spate of books about World War I. The years 1928-1930 produced a bonanza of memoirs, novels, and interpretations, all preaching the futility of war, and the absolute necessity for

INTRODUCTION

survival's sake of avoiding another one. Many of these works studied the origins of the war and concluded that human error and miscalculations were tragically in evidence. The studies of the academicians filtered into the popular mind as a conviction that wars were not started by deliberate acts of aggression or by militaristic designs. Wars were started by mistake or incompetence; it was therefore necessary to keep a wary eye on the politicians and diplomats. Wars were caused by stockpiling armaments; thus the insistence on disarmament as a prerequisite to peace. Wars might be caused by "grievances"; these could be peacefully redressed by mutual accords arrived at in an atmosphere of reason and conciliation. Wars were caused by capitalism or by imperialism which, to Lenin, was the last stage of capitalism. In England, Clement Attlee maintained that so long as there were capitalist governments, they could not be trusted with armaments. So widely held was the belief that World War I had been deliberately fostered by arms manufacturers for private profit that it led to the creation of a royal commission of the War Traffic in England and to a Senate investigation in the United States. Since the established economic and political institutions were by nature hypocritical and self-serving, — whether nominally democratic or totalitarian — one approach of pacifists was to deprive governments of manpower where they might not deprive them of arms. An expression of a profound fatalism occurred in 1933, when the Oxford Union,

INTRODUCTION

voted overwhelmingly for the resolution, "This House will not fight for King and Country."

The feelings of futility so pervasive in the 1930s, the disgust with statesmanship, the disavowal of causes, are fully mirrored in A.A. Milne's Peace with Honour. To Milne, as to so many of his contemporaries, war was a total and unmitigated evil which could no longer be excused by any of the rationales which had served in the past. Honor, prestige, patriotism, all were sentimental labels to cover the duplicity, shallowness, or venality of powerful men: England's honor meant exactly the same as the honor of France or Germany or Italy, where presumably prestige was a reputation for belligerence and patriotism could be defined as a passionate interest in the military strength of one's own country. War, to Milne, was a human creation and could quite simply be eliminated if men would determine never again to go to war no matter what the ostensible provocation. Carrying this logic to its ultimate extreme, Milne does not even believe self-preservation is a valid reason for going to war. The bombs that would be exploded in the name of self-preservation would destroy the defender as surely as it would destroy the attacker — the inescapable paradox of modern warfare.

Since wars could easily be ascribed to incompetent leadership, Milne rather whimsically suggests that upon the outbreak of any new war, the statesmen who either brought on that war, or did not have sufficient wit to prevent it, be put to death. One

INTRODUCTION

concludes that Milne believed that political leaders while sometimes deluded, were basically reasonable individuals who required merely a firm rein and a constant reminder of their own mortality to keep them restrained. Evidently, Milne was unable to entertain the possibility that willful irrationality was a factor in international affairs even to describe the behavior of totalitarian leaders who extolled and reveled in the irrational. He assumed that the Germany of Hitler and the Italy of Mussolini, while verbally bellicose, were basically amenable to reason and anxious for the security of peace: "For, however completely Fascist leaders seem to have forgotten the horrors of the last war, we may be sure that the supreme horror of war is vividly in their minds."

In retrospect, it would seem that Milne was reflecting what had almost become an orthodox viewpoint of the causes of war and their prevention. The mass illusion which induced a kind of double-think, insisted that defense was the same as aggression; that one had only to be persuaded of the awful destructiveness of war to foreswear it; that in the last resort war could be avoided by refusing to fight.

One of the supreme contradictions of the pacifism for which Milne spoke, was that while it distrusted politicians and diplomats, in the absence of a powerful international body or any realistic alternatives for easing the tensions that lead to war, it had to fall back on the same sort of political leadership that had proved so signally inept in the period before World

INTRODUCTION

War I. In Peace with Honour, *Milne has a most revealing fantasy in which he brings together the leaders of the four Western European powers to resolve their grievances by arbitration. Needless to say, the conference between MacDonald, Doumergue, Hitler, and Mussolini is orchestrated by Milne himself in his self-appointed role as the voice of reason. He makes clear that the survival of civilization itself depends solely on their purposefulness and sense of responsibility. Setting forth the priorities, Milne emphasizes that to prevent war, "It is necessary that the renunciation of war must be kept continually in your minds as the first duty of this conference." Once this imperative was perceived, Milne was confident any grievance could be resolved to the satisfaction of all parties.*

It is perhaps a sad commentary on the assumptions of Milne's pacifism that such a conference between the European leaders to resolve grievances did take place in 1938, and that Munich in no way settled the international situation. History which teaches so few lessons seems at least to have made clear that while wars are indeed the result of tragic human failures, the key to their prevention requires more of an understanding of human psychology and human institutions than that overwrought period of the thirties could contemplate.

Sylvia Strauss
Newark State College

PEACE WITH HONOUR

PEACE WITH HONOUR

An Enquiry into the War Convention

by

A. A. MILNE

THIRD EDITION

METHUEN & CO. LTD. LONDON
36 Essex Street W.C.

First published . . *September 27th 1934*
Second Edition . . *October*   *1934*
Third Edition . .   *1934*

PRINTED IN GREAT BRITAIN

PREFACE

I HAVE been considering the writing of this book for many years, and have actually written it in the twelve months from July, 1933 to July, 1934. It is difficult, while writing such a book, not to be carried away by current speeches and events which bear upon one's subject; but I have tried (though not with complete success) to avoid the distraction of the contemporary wrangle and the seduction of the too topical illustration. If, as a result, I have become so out-of-date that I have spoken of a dead man as if he were still alive, or of a dishonoured one as if he still directed our destinies, I have preferred to leave it so (since it does not affect my argument), rather than disfigure the pages with a spray of stop-press footnotes.

Perhaps I should add that throughout I have written of 'Pacifists' and 'Pacifism'. Purists, I am told, write of 'Pacificists' and 'Pacificism'. I have also written of 'England', when Scotsmen would undoubtedly write of 'Great Britain and the North of Ireland'. Whatever else in the book may offend people, I hope that these simple contractions will not be regarded as a further cause of offence. They can hardly be a cause of mystification.

A. A. M.

CONTENTS

CHAP.		PAGE
I	War	1
II	Pacifists All	3
III	England's Honour	12
IV	National Prestige	21
V	National Pride	29
VI	The War Convention	39
VII	The Thin Red Line	47
VIII	Onward, Christian Soldiers	59
IX	Ten Million—and Forty	81
X	'Not Too Pacifist, I Hope'	98
XI	Human Nature	107
XII	Aggression and Defence	122
XIII	Fascist Interlude	135
XIV	Arbitration	146
XV	Notes for a Peace Conference	159
XVI	Patriotism and Pledges	173
XVII	Refusal of War	194
XVIII	'Women and Children First'	208

CHAPTER I
WAR

*I*N *the summer of* 1914 *an Austrian archduke was killed at Serajevo, under, it was said, Servian auspices. Austria's honour, since she was a bigger country than Servia, demanded that she should seek what is called satisfaction. Servia agreed to make certain of the obeisances and motions of humility suggested to her, but rejected certain others. Complete satisfaction being necessary to the honour of Austria, no course was left to her but the forcing of these other obeisances upon the smaller country. The force applied led directly to the killing of ten million men who were not archdukes, and, directly or indirectly, to the deaths of uncounted thousands of women and children. Even so, however, the object remained unachieved. The further obeisances were not made, and four years later Austria was still incompletely satisfied. . . .*

That is the story, told as concisely as possible, of The Great War. I invite my readers to give it their attention. The story has been told more elaborately by other writers, but not more truthfully. All that we need to know of the origins, meaning and purpose of war is given in those hundred and thirty-four words; between those seventeen lines is recorded the whole tragedy of international futility.

CHAPTER II

PACIFISTS ALL

I

EVERY argument between two people is liable to sink, or rise, to the level of a dog-fight. Now the peculiarity of a dog-fight is that at any given moment one is never sure which part of it is one's own dog and which part the other man's. I have heard Pacifist arguing with Militarist, and the ground on which each stood shifted so rapidly that, at the hottest moment of encounter, the only thing which seemed really to be infuriating them was the fact that apparently they were in complete agreement with each other. No one so ardent for peace as Militarist; no one so eager to defend his country as Pacifist. Yet they did not seem very happy about it.

I shall begin, then, by defining my own ground as clearly as possible.

I am against War. President Coolidge, who was a laconic man, was asked by his wife one Sunday what subject the minister had preached upon that morning. He replied 'Sin'. She was eager for details. What line of thought had he followed? What had been his particular message to the congregation? What had he said about Sin? 'He was against it,' said the President briefly. So, and for the same reasons, I am against War. By this I mean that I think war wrong: as I think cruelty to children wrong: as I think slavery and the burning of heretics wrong: as I think the exploitation of the poor wrong, and the corruption of the innocent.

I think war wrong. I also think it silly. Sometimes a comedian in a theatre will do something so divinely irresponsible, so completely and gorgeously silly, that one sinks back into one's seat in helpless laughter. A few minutes later he does it again . . . and then again . . . and again. Gradually one ceases to laugh. So a god, to whom the death of a man was no more than to man the death of a fly, must once have laughed uproariously at man's invention of war . . . and grown weary of laughing . . . and then wished that the absurd little creatures would hit upon something else as gorgeously comic.

I think war silly. I think that war is the ultimate expression of man's wickedness and man's silliness. There are times when I think that its childish silliness is even more heart-breaking than its wickedness.

2

If everybody in Europe thought as I do, there would be no more war in Europe. If a few important people thought as I do: if Ramsay MacDonald were Milne, and Mussolini were Milne, and Stalin were Milne, and Hitler were Milne, and anybody who might at any moment be in a French Cabinet were Milne: then, however intolerable the prospect in other ways, there would be no more war in Europe. If Beaverbrook were Milne, and Rothermere were Milne, and the proprietors of fifty chosen newspapers in Europe were Milne, there would be no more war in Europe. If only the Pope were Milne, and the Archbishop of Canterbury were Milne, then it is at least possible that there would be no more war in Europe.

This does not mean that there is an infallible Milne Plan for abolishing war; it is just a plain statement of fact. War is something of man's own fostering, and if all mankind renounces it, then it is no longer there. Equally, if those particular men who speak for, or order the voices of, the inarticulate were to renounce war, then war would no longer be there. Now when an articulate man feels deeply about anything, he tries, by writing or by preaching, to persuade others into his own way of thinking. In this book I am trying to persuade other people to feel as deeply as I do about war. If everybody reads the book (which is unlikely), and if everybody who reads it is persuaded by it (which is also unlikely), then the thing is done. There is an end of war. I can hope for no such immediate and gratifying response, but at least I can hope that, of the few who read it, a few will be persuaded by it, and will themselves try to persuade others. It is thus that ideas spread, and ultimately influence the world. St. Paul (with whom otherwise, however, I do not compare myself) was not deterred from writing a letter to a few friends at Corinth because he could not foresee the day when it would become the First Epistle to the Corinthians. . . .

At this point an Elder Statesman shows signs of impatience.

But, my dear Sir (he cries), what is this wonderful idea which you are hoping to spread? Whom are you trying to persuade, and to what? Except for a few fire-eaters here and there, we are all in agreement with you. We all know now what war is like and none of us wants 1914 over again. The point which exercises us now is: *How are we going to prevent it?* If by Limitation of Armaments, then how shall we ensure that it is carried out? If by Pacts and Treaties, how shall we enforce them? We all know that modern war is disaster, but what are we going to put in its place?

PACIFISTS ALL

You talk about the Pope and the Archbishop as if you wanted to convert them. Convert them to what? Don't you think that *they* realize the horrors of war? Don't you think that they are just as ardent for Peace as you are? As we all are? Tell us what to *do*, not what to think. We have done our thinking; we are all of one mind as to what we want—Peace; and now the problem in front of us is how to obtain it.

I have typified this imaginary interrupter as an Elder Statesman, but his attitude of mind is common to people of various ages and varying professions. It exhibits the increasingly popular, but mistaken, belief that ' We are all pacifists nowadays '.

We are not.

Consider for a moment the Elder Statesman. For centuries he has been accustomed to think of war as the instrument of policy. Now he sees it suddenly as an instrument as fatal to himself, as fatal to civilization, as to the enemy. Anxiously he wonders how to fashion, from this well-known, well-tried instrument, something less self-destructive. It is as if a mother saw her children playing with a live bomb, and instead of snatching it away from them, said kindly: ' It would be nicer with your proper ball, wouldn't it, darlings? Just go on playing with that one, while Mummy tries to find it for you.' This is not how people behave in their private lives. When a man sees poison in the glass which should have held a tonic, he throws it away. If, being all Pacifists nowadays, we thought that war was poison, we should throw it away. We should not roll it meditatively round the tongue and wonder how to improve the taste. It is because I want everybody to think (as I do) that war is poison, and not (as so many think) an over-strong, extremely unpleasant medicine, that I am writing this book.

For alas! the Great and Good and Wise whom I have mentioned do not think as I do in this matter. The Prime Minister and Sir John Simon think that modern war is disastrous; I think that war is wrong. The Pope and the Archbishop of Canterbury think that modern war is horrible; I think that war is wrong. Lord Beaverbrook and Lord Rothermere think that modern war puts too great a burden on the taxpayer; I think that war is wrong. In short, I think that war is a Bad Thing, and all these gentlemen, and millions like them, think that war is now become Much too Much of a Good Thing.

3

It may be said that, since we all want to end war, it does not greatly matter that we condemn it in different degrees and from differing motives. I think that the realization of these differences is of the first importance to the cause of Peace.

For if there were no differences; if we all wanted the same thing, in the same way, for the same reasons, and with the same ardour, and if we found that we could not set about attaining it with any certainty of ultimate success, we could only conclude that we were striving against some Law of Nature, or of Civilization, which was beyond human control. So, if we all want Peace, and think mistakenly that we want it for the same reasons and with the same ardour, our failure to visualize achievement will force us to the conclusion that the abolition of war is a task of superhuman difficulty.

One can imagine a genuine peace-lover expressing himself like this:

'Well, I've done my best. I always felt uneasy about war, and I only went into the last one because I was assured, and convinced, that it was a war to end war. It seems now that war has got too strong a hold on the world for us ever to end it. For fifteen years we have had all the greatest minds in Europe at work on the problem—and where are we? No nearer to the abolition of war than we were in 1913. In 1913, with a few exceptions, we all thought war was a natural and fine thing to happen, so long as we were well prepared for it and had no doubt about coming out the victor. Now, with a few exceptions, we have lost our illusions ; we are agreed that war is neither natural nor fine, and that the victor suffers from it equally with the vanquished. Yet there seems to be no way of putting an end to it. So what is one to do ? Nothing : except to see that one is as well prepared for the next war as one's neighbour ; nothing : except pray that one will be finished with such a stupid world before Hell opens on it again.'

It is not so hopeless as that. The greatest minds may have been at work, but they have not been single-minded. They have not been determined on Peace ; they have merely been exploring the avenues of Peace with Honour, Peace with Security, Peace with—what you will.

If a man and his wife and his cook and his house-parlourmaid are all determined to have a refrigerator in the house, then in a very short time there is a refrigerator in the house. But if the husband wants a refrigerator, and thinks it ought to come out of the wife's allowance ; and if the wife wants a refrigerator, and doesn't think they can afford it unless the husband gives up smoking ; and if the cook wants it, and sees no place for it but the pantry, and the house-parlourmaid wants it, and sees no place for it but the kitchen ; then, even if years elapse without a refrigerator coming into that house, it will still be a mistake to suppose that refrigerators are not obtainable. . . .

And if, after a lapse of years, it were discovered that, in fact, refrigerators cost nothing and took up no room, this prolonged household discussion about place and price would seem somewhat ironic.

So, to one who holds that without the abolition of war there can be neither Honour nor Security, these prolonged national discussions about Peace with Honour and Peace with Security seem also somewhat ironic.

CHAPTER III

ENGLAND'S HONOUR

I

ONE of the difficulties of thinking clearly about anything is that it is almost impossible not to form our ideas in words which have some previous association for us; with the result that our thought is already shaped along certain lines before we have begun to follow it out. Again, a word may have various meanings, and our use of it in one sense may deceive our readers (or even ourselves) into supposing that we were using it in some other sense. 'Human Nature', for example, may mean 'animal nature', which is merely the instinct for life, or it may mean 'man's spiritual nature', which is the instinct for God. To those who do not appreciate the distinction the statement, made so often in apology for war, 'You can't change human nature', will convey the suggestion that it would be almost sacrilegious to try; whereas, in fact, all human life is, or should be, an attempt of the spiritual nature, which is man's alone, to overcome that animal nature which he shares with the beasts. So, too, with the word 'fight', which can mean anything from a hand-to-hand struggle with a hated opponent down to the acceptance of death from poison-gas at seventy miles range, through the agency, possibly, of an intimate friend.

So, too, with the word 'honour'.

2

In the days before the War, when it was the custom to deride certain pacifically minded men as the Peace-at-any-price Party, it would be emphasized proudly that the only peace which a Patriot could contemplate without repulsion was Peace with Honour. The sentiment still holds.

It sounds noble. All the honourable associations of the word honour rush into our mind. Could an honourable man accept less for his honoured country? We are men of honour! England's honour is at stake! To arms!

Let us, then, consider what a nation means when it talks about its honour.

'What is in that word honour?' asked Falstaff. 'What is that honour? Air.' But this is an opinion rather than a definition. 'Honour', says the dictionary, 'is a fine sense of, and strict allegiance to, what is due and right.' Wordsworth calls it 'the finest sense of justice which the human mind can frame'. All this is very well; but when Lovelace declares that he could not love Althea so much, loved he not honour more; or when any hero in any melodrama cries 'Death rather than dishonour!'—then they seem to give a spiritual implication to the word which takes it beyond the bounds of these definitions. I should prefer to misquote another poet, and say that

> Acting the law we live by without fear,
> And, because right is right, to follow right
> Were honour in the scorn of consequence.

An honourable man, in fact, is he who carries in his heart some ideal of truth, of justice, of beauty which he values above all worldly advantage, and will not surrender even to Death itself. Stevenson speaks of the 'risk of death' as being the touchstone of the noble profession; and by that he meant no more and no less than that nobility is lacking if opportunity be not given 'to follow right in scorn of consequence'. So must the honourable man be prepared to suffer all things rather than be false to the truth within him. Death rather than dishonour.

What, on any of these definitions, is in that phrase a nation's honour; what is that honour? Air.

A nation has no honour. No nation takes willingly the 'risk of death'. No nation suffers all things rather than be false to the truth. No nation shows a strict allegiance to what is due and right. No nation follows right in scorn of consequence.

For a nation has only one law⁻: the Law of Self-Preservation and Self-Advantage. A nation recognizes only one God : Itself.

3

This has not deterred nations from talking vociferously of their honour. It has not prevented them from going to war in defence of their honour. Confidence tricksters also talk loudly of their honour, and prove it by decamping as soon as they have got the money. So, when a nation fights in defence of its honour, it proves its honour by taking the name of God in vain, worshipping false gods and graven images, dishonouring the Sabbath, stealing, murdering, organizing adultery, bearing false witness, and coveting its neighbour's ironfields : thus disposing of nine out of the ten commandments.

Now there is nothing surprising about this. If a nation recognizes no law but the law of self-advancement ; if it regards as its supreme duty the preservation, and, whenever possible, enlargement of its nationhood, then morality and justice can have no meaning for it. Later on we may consider whether a corporate body which, almost inevitably by its own articles of incorporation, is forced to outrage every decent instinct of its members is worth defending, worshipping, preserving; but for the moment I am concerned only with the fact. A nation, being occupied with no higher end than its own existence, has no honour to defend. It has nothing to defend but itself.

Let it be clear that, when I say honour, I mean this inner fortress of the soul. I do not mean prestige; nor that artificial pride to which men of honour made blood-sacrifice in the days of duelling. This pride, this prestige takes its nourishment from without, and only from without can it be harmed. But honour dwells within, and only the keeper of it can do it injury. If a nation were concerned about its honour, it would be concerned about something in its own keeping, which no other nation could challenge; but if a nation is concerned about its prestige, then it is concerned about something which is in the keeping of other nations. War may be necessary to prestige, but never to honour.

I have said that a nation shows its lack of honour in that it will not take the 'risk of death' for an ideal, as will an honourable man. Almost as I was writing these words, my country decided to illustrate them for me. It was announced (appropriately, round about Armistice Day) that, in place of two 8,000-ton cruisers which were to be laid down, two 10,000-ton cruisers would now be built, in order to keep in line with the naval programmes of America and Japan. Let us give this our meticulous attention.

We are at peace with America. We are at peace with Japan. These two countries were our allies in the last war. It is inconceivable that we should ever go to war with America. It is, I suppose, conceivable that on some future occasion we might go to war with our ally, Japan. A cruiser has but a short life before it becomes out-of-date. Conceivably we might go to war with our ally, Japan, within the lifetime of these two cruisers. Conceivably a war might be lost for lack of two cruisers. Conceivably a war might be lost, not for lack of two cruisers, but by reason of a slight deficit in the tonnage of two cruisers. All these things are just conceivable.

Now what is the chance of all these just conceivable things happening in sequence? What is the chance of a war being fought between two allies within the lifetime of two cruisers, and being lost by one of them because of a slight deficit in the tonnage of these two cruisers? One in a hundred? One in a thousand? One in a million? Each of us will put his own figure. But we shall agree that the risk of its happening is an extremely small one. Well, England proclaims continually that she has the ideal of Peace before her; an ideal to be reached, in the opinion of her

Government, through the limitation of armaments. Yet she will not take even this contemptible ' risk of death ' in order to make a gesture towards the ideal.

Or again :

Some months ago China and Japan were at war. While England expressed her condemnation at Geneva, English nationals were busy exporting arms to both combatants. Presumably England's sense of humour rather than her sense of honour was disturbed. Nobly she put an embargo on the exportation of arms, as a shining example to other nations of self-sacrifice in the cause of Peace. Hurriedly, when the example was not followed by other nations, and it looked as though a real sacrifice were being made, she withdrew the embargo. Her nationals were encouraged to go on exporting arms to both combatants in the war which she had condemned.

This is not the way in which decent men and women behave. An honourable man, with money beyond his own needs, does not refuse to help the poor because there is a thousand-to-one chance (as, of course, there is) that he may himself be impoverished one day. He does not refrain from trafficking in opium only if his rivals in business also refrain. But, having considered the two examples above of a nation in action, we realize that any mention to it of the word honour would be almost an indelicacy. The scorn of consequence has no place in matters of policy, nor allegiance to an idea, nor a fine sense of justice. 'And because right is right to follow right'—the words are equally farcical when thought of in connexion with England and with Al Capone; with America and with Horatio Bottomley; with France and Germany and the Leader of the Black Hand. Like these individuals, nations do nothing but for their own advantage.

4

England's honour! One would like to think that it meant something. It is necessary for the Patriot to understand that it means exactly as much as France's honour and Germany's honour and Italy's honour; which is exactly nothing. Abroad we are called Perfidious Albion. We may protest that this exclusive tradition of perfidy is a monstrously unfair invention of jealous competitors. In a sense it is. Yet it may be pointed out that honourable men, however greatly envied, are not known to their neighbours as Perfidious Henry or Perfidious John....

But if, in a gang of crooks, there was one crook, a little less hardened than the others; one crook who announced before each operation that, though he would do his part, his conscience would not allow him to take any share of the swag; who, at the divide-out, said that for form's sake he ought to keep a few bits of glass as a memento . . . and was invariably found to have got away with all the diamonds ; well, we can understand that to his completely depraved companions his depravity would assume a special significance. He might be known as Treacherous Thomas—or something even more colourful.

Let us, then, admit that in the matter of honour we are no better than our neighbours ; or, if we will not admit this, let us acknowledge that they think no more highly of us than we think of them. For the simple truth is that no nation trusts another nation. No nation believes in the good faith of another nation. No nation can give its word of honour to another nation, because no nation has a word of honour to give. It is as meaningless for a nation to talk about its honour as it would be for a cholera germ to talk about its honour ; or a bath-mat ; or the Multiplication Table.

CHAPTER IV

NATIONAL PRESTIGE

I

SINCE we cannot use the word Honour in connexion with national policies, what word shall we substitute ? Let us try Prestige.

By derivation 'prestige' means 'illusion' or 'imposture', and we may find that national prestige is, indeed, no more than this ; but for the moment I use the word in its transferred, and now generally accepted, sense of 'reputation'. To miscall this prestige honour is to invoke all the deep spiritual associations of that word ; to think of it as reputation is to invoke no associations, for the word has no essential meaning. One can have a reputation for cricket or cucumbers, character or chiropody. 'A country's honour' would then mean a reputation for something : something which was not, merely by use of the word honour, in itself honourable. 'Peace with Honour' would mean merely Peace with Unimpaired Prestige.

What is this prestige, or reputation, which is so dear to the Patriot?

2

Politicians are accustomed to say, when thinking imperially, that ' if England lost her Colonies ', or, as they are now called, her Dominions-beyond-the-seas, she would ' sink rapidly to the level of a fifth-rate Power '. Just why this would happen I have never understood. At the moment Germany has no colonies, yet she still has the air of being, not only a powerful, but a greatly feared country. Italy would seem to derive no startling moral or material sustenance from Tripoli or Somaliland, yet, with a population smaller than England's, she maintains an appearance of equality in the councils of Europe. Even without her Colonies England would be superior to most countries in numbers, natural advantages and material wealth ; nevertheless her rapid descent to fifth-rateness would be inevitable. Why?

As I say, I do not know why. I suspect some exaggeration. Probably all that the speaker intends to say is that without her Colonies England would not be so powerful as she is now. But in all the public or private argument which I have heard on this matter ; on all the hundred occasions on which this conditional collapse of England has been heralded ; always the phrase ' fifth-rate

NATIONAL PRESTIGE

Power' has been used—never 'fifth-rate country', never, even, 'fifth-rate nation'.

For once the right, and the most revealing, word has been used.

We talk loosely of 'England', of 'our country'. *England, with all thy faults I love thee still—My country, 'tis of thee—The custom of the country—My country, right or wrong—England, my England—A country's songs and a country's laws.* At one time we mean all of England that has grown up in our hearts from childhood. At another time we mean that corner of England which is Whitehall. At another time we mean no more of England than can be represented by Woolwich Arsenal.

Now it is necessary that we should keep these Englands separate in our minds, so that, when talking of one of them, we shall not, subconsciously, be thinking of the others. The associated memories of the word 'England' (or of the word 'country' as meaning England) are as dangerous to clear thinking as were the associated memories of the word 'honour'. Let us, then, distinguish these three Englands as England the Country, England the Nation and England the Power.

Country . . . Nation . . . Power. With what voices do they speak to us?

A Country speaks to us through her poets and

her painters, her builders long dead and her craftsmen unremembered; her hills and her valleys her woods and streams and meadows ; she speaks with the voices of village church and of village green. We love her ; we dare not talk of her ; she whispers to us and we cannot pass the secret on. Calling us with a thousand voices she remains inarticulate ; we know no more than that she is England, we are English, this is Home.

A Nation has one clear voice. It speaks to us through its mouthpiece the national Government of the day. It orders our justice ; it makes our laws ; it preserves, or should preserve, the amenities ; it encourages, or should encourage, the arts.

A Power is a Nation speaking to other Nations. The Forest of Arden . . . Whitehall . . . Woolwich Arsenal. . . .

Now you will notice that whenever a Patriot (who may be loosely defined as a man who thinks that other people are not patriots) talks about England, he means always this third England, the Great Power. He is not thinking of the England of Shakespeare and Dickens, and calling his neighbour a traitor for preferring the pleasures of Tchehov and Dostoievsky. He is not thinking of English government, and extolling democracy over fascism. He is thinking of England as a nation in competition with other nations : of England, that is, as a Power.

NATIONAL PRESTIGE

What is a Great Power? There can be no argument about that. Powers are reckoned as Great or Small, according to their capacity for war.

So, when the Patriot cries that England's prestige is in danger, he means that England's reputation as a Great Power is in danger; by which he means only this: that England's reputation for war-capacity is in danger.

3

Englishmen are proud of their country's reputation. She has, they like to think, a reputation for liberty of thought and speech, something which is very dear to most of them. She has a reputation for the purity of her justice, and that also is dear to them. She has a reputation, though perhaps only a comparative reputation, for the incorruptibility of her officials. She has a reputation for inspiring great literature; a reputation for fostering humour and stubbornness and a cheerful acceptance of ill-fortune.

In international affairs, when England is playing her part as a Great Power, none of these reputations is at hazard, nor needs to be defended by arms. It is merely her reputation as a belligerent which is in danger—her prestige as a fighting nation determined to 'stand no nonsense' (even if it means the death of ten million human beings) from any other nation.

Let us keep this fact clearly in our minds. Whether he use the word 'honour' or the word 'prestige', the Patriot means exactly this: his country's reputation for getting what she wants, or defending what she has got, by force of arms.

Now there is this interesting fact to be noted about national prestige. Not only can the prestige of a Power suffer nothing at the hands of a recognizably greater Power, but it is most in jeopardy at the hands of a recognizably smaller Power. If, for instance, a Spanish mob attacked the British Embassy in Madrid, and murdered the residents, the British patriot would feel that the national prestige could only be upheld by immediate armed invasion of Spain. But if a similar attack were made upon the British Embassy in Paris, an armed invasion of France would seem the less necessary to England's prestige in proportion to its greater hazard. And, obviously, if the Spanish Embassy were attacked by a London mob, not even the proudest Spanish patriot would feel that an immediate invasion of England was necessary to his country's honour.

It is true that a Small Power has occasionally defied a Great Power (as in the cases of Servia, Belgium and the Boer Republics), but the Small Power will almost inevitably be found to have behind it, either the assurance of help from some other Great Power, or else the confidence of hidden

NATIONAL PRESTIGE

resources against which, it is believed, the Great Power will battle in vain. No nation goes to war —defends, that is, its prestige—with the probability of defeat in front of it; as in duelling days men faced almost certain death to defend what they thought of as their honour.

Prestige, then, is a reputation for belligerence. I have called it a reputation for war-capacity, but actually the capacity for war is not enough. There must also be the 'will to war'. Potentially America has always had the greatest war-capacity in the world, but her President's famous declaration in 1915 that she was too proud to fight only brought her the contempt of other nations. America was in no danger from Germany; could never be in danger from Germany; and if she joined the Allies, she was certain of joining the winning side. Consequently her prestige demanded that she should join the winning side. An individual may be too proud to fight; too proud to reply to insult from one to whom he holds himself superior. But nations do not go in for that sort of pride.

4

To sum up:

When a nation talks of its honour, it means its prestige. National prestige is a reputation for the will to war. A nation's honour, then, is measured by a nation's willingness to use force to maintain its reputation as a user of force. If one could imagine the game of tiddleywinks assuming a supreme importance in the eyes of statesmen, and if some innocent savage were to ask *why* tiddleywinks was so important to Europeans, the answer would be that only by skill at tiddleywinks could a country preserve its reputation as a country skilful at tiddleywinks. Which answer might cause the savage some amusement.

CHAPTER V

NATIONAL PRIDE

I

AT this point I shall assume further signs of impatience from the Elder Statesman.

He says :

I have followed your argument closely. As I understand it, you have suggested that, when a nation talks of its honour, it means no more than its prestige ; and that, when it talks of its prestige, it means no more than its reputation for belligerence ; whence it follows that, unless belligerence is a noble end in itself (which only the most confirmed militarist would venture to suggest), honour and prestige are illusory words as used between nations. But even if this be accepted, has it any value, save on the assumption that wars are only waged in defence of a country's honour or in assertion of a country's prestige ? Is it not the fact, rather, that nearly all wars have a material motive ? The end and purpose of war is economic advantage : the acquisition or defence of territory, the removal of tariff barriers, the concession of trading-rights, the opening-up of harbours and waterways. Then how can you abolish war merely by proving that the spiritual motive amounts to nothing of value?

Now it is true that the purpose of war is usually economic advantage. There is, however, a noticeable difference between an ultimatum and a battle. A war may have an undoubted, undisguised economic motive in the minds of the statesmen who declare it; but wars are not fought by statesmen. They are fought by common people. Before common people rush to the defence of their country (stopping for a moment in the Mall to sing *God Save the King*) they have to be roused emotionally. No doubt the news that a million gold coins had been dropped in the Mall would rouse almost anybody emotionally, and send him hurrying down the Duke of York's steps to the battlefield. But the economic motive of war is not so simple as this. If the common man has ever understood fully, and pondered over, the particular economic motive for an ultimatum, he has been absolutely certain of one thing: that however greatly any group of politicians, financiers captains of industry or armament kings may be going to profit by a war, he himself is not going to make one penny out of it. He is getting £5 a week now; and if he survives the war (which is doubtful), and finds his job still waiting for him (which is improbable) then, even though 1,000,000 square miles and twenty oil-fields be added to the Empire, he will, at the end of the war, still be getting £5 a week, and paying twice as much in taxes for it.

No. Wars may be declared for economic reasons, but they are fought by volunteers for sentimental reasons. However loudly an iron-field may call to the Elder Statesman, the call will come to Youth through the voices of King and Country. And even the most cynical statesman would hesitate to tell the young volunteer that his King and Country needed him in order to make a certain corner of the world safe for speculators.

But are wars even declared entirely for economic reasons? Is not the statesman also subject to the sentimental impulse? If his motives were purely economic, one would expect him to make out a balance-sheet before he issued his ultimatum; taking into account, on the credit side the value of the oil-fields, gold-fields, iron-fields, or whatever was the gleam which he was following; and, on the debit side, the probable length of the war, the estimated cost per day, the estimated number of casualties (and consequent cost of pensions), depreciation of stock, insurance against defeat, damage inflicted by aeroplanes, and so forth. He makes no such balance-sheet. It may be said that he hopes to get his expenses back by way of indemnity, just as a suitor in the law-courts hopes to get his costs. Well, he has discovered by now that indemnity on that scale is simply unpayable ; but, even before this great and (one would have thought) elementary discovery was made, there still remained, on the debit side of the account, the irreplaceable human lives. Are the economic gains of war ever balanced against dead Englishmen ? Against human misery ? It would hardly seem so. The economics of the war-minded statesman are the economics of the nursery. A baby putting its hand into the fire to take out the pretty coal shows as much awareness of reality.

For the truth is this. A nation may declare war in pursuit of some material end, yet, in reality, it is declaring war at the call of ' honour '. Because ' *honour* ' *demands that a nation shall achieve its ends regardless of cost.*

2

This ' honour ', as I have shown, is nothing honourable. It is merely the artificial pride of the duellist. In the days when duelling was the fashion men fought because they ' had to fight ' ; because honour compelled them to fight ; because they were too proud not to fight.

Now it is almost impossible for Pacifist and

Militarist to get into argument about war without the analogy of the duel being brought up, sooner or later, by one or other of them. It might be as well, then, now that I have likened the motive of war to the motive of the duel, to follow the analogy through to the end.

Twenty years ago the comparison between private war and international war was often made. 'Consider', the pacifist's argument ran, 'how ridiculous the idea of abolishing duelling must have seemed once—as ridiculous as seems now the idea of abolishing war. But the world progresses; and if we have got rid of the one, why should we not get rid of the other?' To which came the inevitable militarist answer: 'We got rid of duelling because we had an over-riding authority which could call duellists to account; but it is impossible to create an over-riding authority which can call nations to account.'

Since those days the League of Nations was conceived, has come into being, and now waits uncertainly on its future.

Yet the argument remains. And the argument is not: Since national law has enforced the abandonment of duelling, therefore international law could enforce the abandonment of war; but simply: Since we have outgrown the one convention, is there any reason why we should not outgrow the other?

It is true that, if I fight a duel with a man who has insulted me, I shall be put in prison, and that if I kill him, I shall be hanged; it is true that, however much I wanted to fight him, the certainty of imprisonment, and the probability that one way or the other I should lose my own life, would prevent me from challenging him. But the more profound truth is that I no longer want to fight him. And the reason that I do not want to fight him is not because I am afraid of the consequences, but because the whole idea of fighting seems now to be ridiculous. The duelling convention, in fact, has ceased to exist.

Is there any necessity for the war-convention to continue? We have outgrown the one convention, why should we not outgrow the other?

For this reason (says the Elder Statesman). There is always an intermediary period when an idea is not strong enough to flourish by itself, but needs protection; just as young grass needs protection in between the time when it is sown and the time when it is established. In the case of duelling this protection was given by the Law, and under the Law the idea that private war was wrong and foolish grew to its present strength But in the case of international war we are back again at the old problem. By what Law, and by what sanctions, can we protect the idea of Peace until it is so firmly established in the minds of

NATIONAL PRIDE

nations that international war seems both wicked and ridiculous?

To give an example (the Elder Statesman goes on). Many of us hate the convention of 'tipping', yet we struggle against it in vain. But if tipping were made illegal and punishable, then in a generation or two the thought of tipping would seem as ridiculous as duelling now seems, and the law against it would never need to be invoked. Yet without the initial aid of the Law we are helpless.

Let us consider the argument and the analogy.

It is true that we should all like to abolish the tip, the gratuity, the *pourboire*. It is true that without the aid of the Law we are not likely to abolish it. It is true that if tipping were made a penal offence, the habit of it would die out, and in a very short time we should wonder that it had ever existed. All of which, it may be argued, is equally true of the war-habit. But is this all the truth? What is 'the aid of the Law' exactly? How in fact does the Law function?

The Law is made and enforced by the Government. The Government is, in theory, the voice of the Nation. When the Law says 'Thou shalt not tip', then, in theory, forty million English people are saying 'We will not tip'. Any one man can say this for himself whenever he likes. Any group of a dozen men can call themselves the Anti-tipping League and pledge themselves against gratuities. Obviously they will suffer for it. They will be marked men in all those places where hopeful hands are held out. But if the League had, not twelve, but twelve million members, then they would not be marked men; they would not suffer for it.

Now the unfortunate thing is that twelve million men cannot get into one room and agree about anything, however much they are of the same mind. If the adult population of England could meet in the Albert Hall, and a vote against tipping be put, and (as is probable) carried unanimously, then tipping in England would be abolished, without the assistance of the Law. This being impossible, what the Law does is to assume, and announce, that unanimous meeting. The Law's assistance to the Cause is, not so much the infliction of penalties against those who betray the Cause, as the official proclamation to the whole of the country that the Cause is in being. It is for lack of that official proclamation that a Cause (whether it be the Abolition of the Duel or the Abolition of Tipping) is unable to make progress; each individual being uncertain of the support of his fellows.

Now the Peace of Europe is in the hands of half a dozen nations. Each of these nations can be, and is, represented by an individual. And it is quite possible for those six individuals to meet in a room, and, even if they are not eloquent in each other's languages, to come to any agreement they please. No over-riding Law, no international Government, is necessary to make the official proclamation that they are agreed. They need no official reassurance. They can see for themselves, they can hear for themselves, that they are agreeing. If those six individuals are in earnest about the Cause, then the Cause is won.

3

To sum up:

1. War is the conventional use of force to satisfy some national ambition regardless of consequences.

2. Wars are usually declared in pursuit of some material end, but no attempt is made to balance the gains of war against the losses, nor to bring into the account the possibility that the end, in fact, will not be attained.

3. The motive which inspires materially minded nations to act in this reckless and uneconomic way is variously described as 'honour', 'patriotism', or 'the necessity of maintaining the national prestige', and is analogous to the 'honour' of the duellist.

4. This honour over-rides every restraining motive of prudence or humanity.

5. Being entirely conventional, it can be renounced—
    (*a*) Without spiritual loss to civilization.
    (*b*) Without regret or misgiving on the part of any national, provided that the renunciation is universal.
    (*c*) Without difficulty, since this renunciation can be agreed upon by a few representative individuals.

CHAPTER VI

THE WAR CONVENTION

I

I HAVE called war 'the conventional use of force' to attain an end. A Pacifist is generally assumed to be a poor-spirited creature who objects to any use of force in any circumstances whatever, and it is customary to ask him, by way of challenge, what he would do if England were invaded and a Storm Trooper tried to rape his mother. Why elderly mothers should have this special (and surely rather surprising) attraction for an invading soldiery, I do not know. Nor do I know what, in the circumstances, the passionate militarist would do, nor why, in the midst of war's alarms, he should be by his mother's side to do it. Least of all do I know why this particular challenge is always issued to the Pacifist. I should have supposed that, since rape was so inevitably one of the accompaniments of war as to be almost the natural perquisite of the invading soldier; and since the passionate militarist, in accepting war, accepts with complaisance the prospect of other people's mothers being raped; it is he rather than the Pacifist who should be asked the question. And asked it, not rhetorically, but with genuine interest. But assuming (as I think we may) that he makes a pious distinction between his own mother and other people's mothers, and that his acceptance of rape is general and patriotic rather than particular, then we may suppose that, instinctively and by the use of force, he would try to prevent the catastrophe. And one pacifist, at least, would applaud him.

But he would be applauding a special instance of an instinctive use of force. War, I have suggested, is a conventional use of force on all occasions which is now become ridiculous.

The parable in the next section, narrating though it does a highly improbable story, shows as clearly as it is possible for me to show, the difference between this instinct and this convention.

2

There was a certain man who was Owner of a garden in which he took great happiness. He delighted in it at all seasons of the year, but most of all he loved it in early May, for in May came the tulips, flowers which to him were the chief glory of the garden. All through the winter he lived for the beauty which was coming to him in May. All through the long winter as he waited for the first reluctant leaves to show; all through the first faint days of Spring, as he watched bed and border slowly begin to take pattern; always he told himself that in this or that number of weeks the glory would be consummated, and his garden filled with that orderly riot of colour which was his great delight.

There came an Intruder: a man who hated gardens; or hated the Owner of the Garden; or perhaps just hated all beautiful things. One April afternoon he came into the garden, and walked round the borders, slashing at the heads of the tulips as he went. And the Owner lay in a chair (for it was a pleasantly warm afternoon) and watched him as he walked up and down destroying all this promise of beauty.

And he wondered what he should do.

Well, what shall he do? Let us consider possible courses of conduct for him.

He might, if he were that sort of man, adopt a completely pacific attitude, turning, as it were, the other cheek to the intruder. He might tell himself that the poor fellow evidently got but little pleasure out of life, and could not decently be interrupted now that he had found at last a means of enjoying himself. He might say: 'Excuse me, sir, but there are a couple of tulips at the back there which you appear to have overlooked. They still hold their heads high. Ah, that's got them.' He might then point out the rock garden as a profitable ground for action when the tulips were finished.

Or he might, being a man of logical mind, and conscious that force is no argument, try the effect of reason. ' Let us, my dear sir,' he might say, ' discuss the matter together, laying all our cards upon the table. Here, upon the one hand, am I, the undoubted owner of all these tulips. Indeed I still have, and shall be happy to produce for your inspection, the receipt for the bulbs from which they sprang. Here, upon the other hand, are you, the undoubted owner of a strong arm and a fine malacca cane. . . .' And with every development of the argument another dozen tulips would lose their heads. . . .

Or he might, being a moral law-abiding citizen, convinced that it is the State's business to see that justice is done between individuals, hurry into the house and ring up the village policeman. Probably the intruder would have departed, his work of destruction done, by the time the policeman arrived. If so, he could then avail himself of the further services of the Law. He could bring an action against his enemy, claiming heavy damages for the destruction of his flowers. He could prosecute him for trespass. But alas! this will not give the tulips back their heads, nor will any money compensate him for the loss of all the beauty which May was to have brought him.

So, if he really loves his garden, he will not do any of these things.
But what else *can* he do?
What he wants to do, what all his instincts tell him to do, what he knows to be the only thing worth doing, is to rush at the intruder and punch him and punch him and punch him, and then turn him round and kick him and kick him and kick him, and, having kicked him as far as the boundary of the garden, to pick the fellow up and hurl him into the road from which he came. . . .
But (as it happens) he cannot do this. For recently he has had the misfortune to break his leg, and now he lies out in his chair in this sunny corner of the garden, unable to move, and forced to watch helplessly the massacre of his tulips. Yet he is not quite helpless. For on the table by his side (never mind why, but let us say, if you like, that his two little children, playing round a rubbish-heap, found it there and brought it to him) lies a live bomb. He has but to take the pin out and jerk the bomb a few yards across the grass, and the work of destruction will be stayed.
Stayed, that is, as far as the intruder is con-

cerned. But obviously the bomb itself will carry on the work of destruction over a considerable part of the garden.

And it will blow the intruder to pieces.

And it will blow the owner to pieces.

And it will blow to pieces the owner's two children, who are pattering behind this exciting visitor.

Does he, then, throw the bomb?

Remember: it is the *only* thing he can do. It is the *only* way in which he can stop this unwarrantable outrage, this horrible vandalism, this hideous affront, this——

Does he throw the bomb?

Of course not.

Would any man in possession of his senses, aware of the consequences, would any man alive in the world to-day throw the bomb?

Of course not.

3

But we can just imagine, can we not, a lunatic world, peopled, not by real men, but by sentimentally obsessed idiots, in which it would be the conventionally heroic thing to throw the bomb; a world in which all the pride of the Cholmondeley-Bolmondeleys called upon a man to assert his manhood at whatever cost in the face of such an insult. We can imagine a lunatic world in which consequence was of no account ; a world in which the destruction which would follow one's action : the death of another man, the suicide of oneself, the mangled bodies of one's children, the agonies of one's wife : all this would be as nothing to the virility and the grandeur and the glory of the action itself. In this lunatic world we can hear the very words, the very tones, in which the poor-spirited creature who rebelled against the convention would be scorned.

' If you don't throw your bomb, what *are* you going to do ? . . . *Nothing ?* . . . My dear man, haven't you any self-respect at all ? '

' Of course I hate mangling little children as much as you do, but one must face realities. In the world as it is to-day . . .'

' Anyhow, you must admit that it takes some courage to sacrifice oneself like that.'

' Well, if one didn't make it quite clear that one wouldn't stand for that sort of thing, it would mean that *anybody* could walk into one's garden and smash it up.'

' Yes, of course it's horrible, but the world's full of horrible things. Look at all the little children who get run over in the streets.'

' After all, it's better than dying of cancer. . . .'

' But damn it, man, haven't you any *pride* ? Doesn't the honour of the Cholmondeley-Bolmondeleys mean *anything* to you ? Do you mean to say that you would lie there and let a confounded Watson-Watson walk into your garden. . . .'

And so on, and so on, and so on.

It is in this lunatic world of the sentimentally obsessed that the war-convention flourishes.

CHAPTER VII

THE THIN RED LINE

I

WE must now face the fact that the war-convention has built up for itself a tradition of sentiment behind which, not only can it repel attack, but fly the flag which makes attack seem almost an outrage.

Listen:

'*Arm, arm, it is the cannon's opening roar!*'

'*The combat deepens: On, ye brave,
Who rush to glory or the grave!*'

'*Battle's magnificently stern array.*'

'" *Charge, Chester, charge! On, Stanley, on!* "
Were the last words of Marmion.'

'*The trumpet, the gallop, the charge, and the
   might of the fight.*'

'*Ten thousand swords leaping from their scabbards.*'

PEACE WITH HONOUR

' How can man die better
Than facing fearful odds ? '

' " Qui procul hinc ", *the legend's writ,*
   The mountain grave lies far away,
" Qui ante diem periit,
   " Sed miles, sed pro patria ".'

Through the mists of emotion which rise from such stirring words as these, war can be comfortably seen as one long procession of Academy pictures : Heroes galloping, sword in hand—Heroes with bandages round their head—Heroes defending the bridge. It is true that in modern warfare swords do not leap from their scabbards to any extent ; it is true that the last words of a commander-in-chief, well back at the base, are never ' Charge, Thompson, charge ! On, Jenkins, on ! ' Yet subconsciously we still think of war as of an infinitude of gallant hand-to-hand combats, in which God, even if He does not monotonously defend the Right, will at least ensure for the loser the consolation of having died for it. Subconsciously we picture each separate hero unsheathing a bright and eager sword for England ; and when on occasion some urgent manœuvre draws them patriotically ' shoulder to shoulder ', the gold-mounted *Steady, the Buffs* in the drawing-room, or the coloured supplement of *The Thin Red Line*

THE THIN RED LINE

in the cook's bedroom, keeps the romantic image splendidly alive.

Some will say that this sentimental view of battle may have survived the Boer War, but that it definitely perished in 1914. We all know that war has ceased to be an affair of flashing swords and charging cavalry.

We know, yes; but we seem to be unable to adapt our minds to the knowledge.

We know, for instance, that, of the casualties of the last war, not all were killed on the battlefield; that hundreds of thousands died painfully of wounds—in bed; that hundreds of thousands died slowly of gas-poisoning or disease—in bed. Yet the sentimentalist, knowing this, still visualizes death in war as something which comes cleanly and swiftly and mercifully, leaving its victim no more time for awareness than is necessary for a last message to his mother. He can still say, in apology for war, that, since death comes to all, at least it is better to be killed on the battlefield than to die lingeringly in bed.

We know that, as a result of the British blockade in the last war, a million women and children in Central Europe died of starvation. Yet the sentimentalist, with the manly names of Inkerman and Rorke's Drift ringing in his ears, can still say that at least a soldier's war is a more humane and gentlemanly business than an economic war of tariffs.

We know, many of us from personal experience, just what the last war was like. Yet, moved by some head-line from Geneva, the meekest little husband will brush the egg off his moustache, and talk of ' the tiger and the ape ' in man, and of man's fierce need to express this fighting spirit ; knowing, if he could but assimilate his memories, that the last war would have failed to satisfy the most inexigent tiger, or the simplest-minded ape just up from the country, and that only its abundant opportunities for lice-hunting would have brought content even to the smaller monkeys.

And when the sentimentalist is not thinking of war in terms of ' Horatius Keeping the Bridge ' or ' Wilson's Last Stand ' he is thinking of it in terms of his regimental tie. War may be hell, but its aftermath is one long and glorious Old Boys Dinner. The friendships it makes ! The memories it gives ! The wonderful way in which it brings the classes together ! A million women may be anguished, a million children raped, starved or blown to pieces . . . but what matter if ex-Captain Wilbraham and ex-Corporal Pennycuick can greet each other in the Strand ten years later : ' Corporal Pennycuick, by all that's holy ! '—' Why, lumme, if it isn't the Captain ! '

2

And then, on Armistice Day, there are the heroic dead to be commemorated. The usual speeches are made, the usual sermons preached, the usual leading articles written, and from every one of these threnodies, however pacific in intention, the suggestion escapes that to fight for one's country is the noblest form of self-expression, to die for one's country the noblest form of self-immolation. Our heroic dead, our immortal dead. *Dulce et decorum est pro patria mori.*

Yet, looking at the matter in the cold light of reason, we see that a man is not a hero who is conscripted; or who is in the army for lack of other employment; or who is carried away by the waving of flags and the thrumming of bands; or who joins up, as so many did, because life in war-time is hell anyway, and only in uniform can one escape from thinking about it. Nor, we observe, do these ordinary unheroic men become heroes just because an incompetent commander has hurled them in mass upon uncut wire, there to hang like blackberries until they are ripe for the honour, if Chance picks upon them, of Unknown Warrior. Alive or dead, they retain the nobility or ignobility of character which was theirs in peace-time; just as the young men of to-day, who have not yet had a war arranged for them, are noble and ignoble.

This sentimental feeling that war is an exhibition of heroism, which grants diplomas to all who attend it, is far from the truth. The whole conception of modern war is almost comically unheroic. Gone are the days of Agincourt when King Harry ' would not lose so great an honour as one man more from England would share from him '. Gone are the days when the little ships of England ranged themselves proudly, almost contemptuously, against the invincible Armada. Gone are the days when a fight was hardly a fight to an Englishman if the odds against him were less than three to one. To-day, with no war in sight, yet in terror lest we should be outbuilt, we seek to match ship for ship, gun for gun, aeroplane for aeroplane ; and even so, when the war comes, it will be the ' gentlemen in England ', the chemists and the munition workers, upon whom victory will depend.

But though modern war is not heroic in itself, it might be urged that those who fall in war fall for a cause outside themselves, and, by so doing, have made, as the threnodists say, the supreme sacrifice : they have given their lives for others. Well, let us continue to be unsentimental. Self-sacrifice, to be heroic, must be a voluntary sacrifice and a deliberate sacrifice. Not more than 5 per cent. of the soldiers in the last war volunteered to fight. Those who did volunteer went into action knowing that casualties would be suffered, but thinking and hoping and praying (so unheroic are the ordinary people who die in war) that the casualties would be, not to themselves but to their companions. They took the risk of death willingly, as young fools take it daily on motor-bicycles, as men take it in aeroplanes, or in search of a Pole, or after big game, or among the mountains; but the absolute certainty of death is something far removed from this. A man is indeed a hero if, longing for life, he accepts death of his own will. How many heroes do we commemorate each year? How many of the 'immortal dead' have deliberately died for their country?

Neither in its origins nor in its conduct is war heroic. Splendidly heroic deeds are done in war, but not by those responsible for its conduct, and not exclusively and inevitably by the dead. Of the ten million men who were killed in the last war, more than nine million had to fight whether they wanted to or not, and of these nine million some eight million did nothing heroic whatever before they were killed. They are no more 'immortal' than a linen-draper who is run over by a lorry; their deaths were no more 'pleasant' and 'fitting' than the death of a stock-broker in his bath.

But of course one can't just say to a million mothers: 'I want your sons', and then six months later: 'Sorry, they're all dead.' If war is to be made tolerable, the romantic tradition must be handed on. 'Madam, I took away your son, but I give you back the memory of a hero. Each year we will celebrate together his immortal passing. *Dulce et decorum est pro patria mori.*'

3

There was a quiet boy in our reserve battalion, fresh from school; the younger of two sons. We went out to France together to join the same service battalion of the regiment, and on the way over I got to know him a little more closely than was possible before. His elder brother had been killed a few months earlier, and he, as the only remaining child, was rather pathetically dear to his father and mother. Indeed (and you may laugh or cry as you will), they had bought for him an under-garment of chain-mail, such as had been worn in the Middle Ages to guard against unfriendly daggers, and was now sold to over-loving mothers as likely to turn a bayonet-thrust or keep off a stray fragment of shell; as, I suppose, it might have done. He was much embarrassed by this parting gift, and though, true to his promise, he was taking it to France with him, he did not know whether he ought to wear it. I suppose that, being fresh from school, he felt it to be ' unsporting'; something not quite done; perhaps, even, a little cowardly. His young mind was torn between his promise to his mother and his hatred of the unusual. He asked my advice: charmingly, ingenuously, pathetically. I told him to wear it; and to tell his mother that he was wearing it; and to tell her how safe it made him feel, and how certain of coming back to her. I do not know whether he took my advice. There was other, and perhaps better, counsel available when we got to our new battalion. Anyway it didn't matter; for on the evening when we first came within reach of the battle-zone, just as he was settling down to his tea, a crump came over and blew him to pieces. . . .

Dulce et decorum est pro patria mori.

But just why it was a pleasant death and a fitting death I still do not understand. Nor, it may be, did his father and mother; even though assured by the Colonel that their son had died as gallantly as he had lived, an English gentleman.

4

It is difficult to work passionately for peace if, at the back of your mind, you feel that war is a gallant exercise, worthy to be sung by poets, which carries with it nothing for tears but an heroic death upon the battlefield. Ruskin, whose military experience must have included several drawing-room renderings of *The Charge of the Light Brigade*, is quoted proudly by an apologist for war as having said that 'all the greatest qualities of man come out in armed conflict'. One might be excused for thinking so after listening to that stirring ballad.

> Forward the Light Brigade !
> Was there a man dismayed ?
> Not tho' the soldier knew
>   Someone had blundered :
> Theirs not to make reply,
> Theirs not to reason why,
> Theirs but to do and die :
> Into the valley of Death
>   Rode the six hundred.

Put like this, even the blundering (which comes out, so monotonously, in armed conflict) seems to earn its place among 'the greatest qualities of man', for, if not heroic in itself, it is at least the cause of heroism in others. 'Theirs not to reason why '—how finely *Homo Sapiens* exhibits his quality.

And yet . . .

If in the last four years 10,000 *Titanics* in succession had struck icebergs and gone to the bottom, each with a loss of a thousand lives, would any moderately sane person, in excuse for doing nothing but build more *Titanics* and crash into more icebergs, utter the complacent truth that all the greatest qualities of man come out in shipwreck?

And has the fact that the greatest qualities of man undoubtedly came out in the Great Plague ever been advanced as an apology for bad sanitation?

And, looking on the bright side of earthquakes, can we not say that all the greatest qualities of man come out in earthquakes?

But most nobly, most gloriously, with a splendour which almost dazzles the sight, the greatest qualities of man have shone forth under religious persecution. Hail, then, rack! Hail, thumbscrew! Bring torches to the faggots, and let the brave fires of Smithfield burn merrily again. *Dulce et decorum est pro Christo mori.*

A hundred years ago a clergyman of the Church of England had the surprising courage to write:

' The greatest curse which can be entailed upon mankind is a state of war. All the atrocious crimes committed in years of peace—all that is spent in peace by the secret corruptions or by the thoughtless extravagances of nations—are mere trifles compared with the gigantic evils which stalk over the world in a state of war. God is forgotten in war—every principle of Christian charity trampled upon.'

But that was a hundred years ago; and the writer, being Sydney Smith, had a considerable reputation as a humorist.

CHAPTER VIII

ONWARD, CHRISTIAN SOLDIERS

I

WHICH is the truth about war: Ruskin's or Sydney Smith's? If Sydney Smith is right in saying ' God is forgotten in war—every principle of Christian charity trampled upon ', it seems strange that Christianity has not yet had the faith or the courage to repudiate war. Right and Wrong are not just distinctions made for our children, so that the house can be kept quiet for Father to enjoy his sleep on a Sunday afternoon; nor are they high-sounding synonyms for Convenience and Inconvenience. Whether he base his faith on the Ten Commandments or the Sermon on the Mount, the Christian is pledged to some ultimate standard of reference by which he conducts his life. If the conduct of his life is to include excursions into ' armed conflict ', he must bring armed conflict to the measure of his own standard.

In this chapter, then, I propose to bring the war-convention to the measure of Christianity.

If, at times, I seem to be exhorting, cross-examining, reproaching the churches, and, more particularly, the Church of England ; if, throughout, I seem to be assuming, both in my readers and myself, an acceptance of orthodox beliefs, it is only because, in the first case, the Church is the official exponent of Right and Wrong, and because, in the second case, a belief in Right and Wrong is, for my present purpose, the only orthodoxy which matters. When I speak of a Christian, I speak of anyone who finds in Christ's teaching his ideal of goodness.

The Churches have accepted war in just the way in which they have accepted epidemic disease. Nobody likes, or encourages, an outbreak of typhoid fever in his village, but, as the Vicar will point out in his next sermon, these trials are sent to us by God. In a particular case, of course, the trial may be attributed, more directly, to the neglect of a landlord or the wilful ignorance of the cottagers. If so, all good men will condemn the landlord or the cottagers. But although at times we are responsible for it, although at times we can prevent it, and always we can fight it, yet disease is an integral part of the world into which God has put us ; and an outbreak of typhoid fever, however regrettable, is not necessarily a matter either for repentance or for remorse.

Just so do the Churches regard war. A particular war in which one's own country is engaged may be attributed to the wickedness of the enemy ; a particular war in which two other countries are engaged may be attributed to the wickedness of both countries. Wicked things are done in war ; by individuals (alas !) of all nations, and by the Governments of all nations but one's own. We should do our utmost, therefore, to prevent war. But an outbreak of war, however regrettable, is not *necessarily* a matter either for repentance or for remorse. War is an integral part of the world into which God has put us.

In short, whenever official Christianity has condemned a war, it has condemned *a* war. Not war.

In the first chapter of this book I described a war. Official Christianity condemned it unsparingly. English Christianity denounced the wickedness of Germany as fearlessly as German Christianity denounced the wickedness of England and the wickedness of Russia. Actually, the war would seem to have been started by Austria ; but the Viennese are a gay people, their music is light and tuneful, and it was charitable to assume that they didn't quite know what they were up to. Even so, however, Servian Christianity spoke out finely on the subject. Let us, then, leave this particular war on which official Christianity has delivered its verdict, and consider a typical war. In fact, the war-convention.

Two nations are in dispute about something. One has it and the other claims it. Or neither has it and both claim it. It seems to be, and may in fact be, to the material advantage of either to enforce possession of it. They talk; they threaten; but neither will give way. A 'state of war' is thereupon declared between them. From this moment a contest begins in which it is the aim of the nationals of one country to kill and mutilate, by certain agreed methods, as many as possible of the nationals of the other country, ignoring for this purpose any of God's commandments which seem to stand in the way. Incident to the contest, and accidental in the sense that a combatant, an explosive or a policy has gone farther than was officially intended, are the rape, the blowing to pieces and the starvation of women and children in carefully unrecorded numbers. The contest (it is understood beforehand) is won by the nation whose Government accepts the slaughter of its men, women and children with the greater fortitude, and it is naturally a matter for constant prayer among the faithful that the slaughter of the opposing nationals shall be so intensified by God's help as to become beyond bearing. When, after a lapse of months or years, the fortitude of one Government gives way, the Government of the winning nation settles the original cause of dispute by taking as much of the loser's wealth or territory as it can profitably assimilate. . . .

This is war. No Church condemns it. Bishops approve heartily of it. Accredited Chaplains accompany the combatants to see that the religious side of their life is not neglected.

What does it all mean? Does one laugh or does one cry?

2

I said in an earlier chapter of this book that I wanted to make people think as I do about war. What I am really trying to make them do is to think again, *and from the beginning*, about war. So many of our beliefs are traditional beliefs which we have inherited without examination. The torture of prisoners until they confessed to a crime which they had not committed used to be accepted by Christians as natural, time-hallowed, approved of God. It seems now as if they were mistaken. If they have also been mistaken all these years about war, it need not be a matter for shocked surprise. The wisdom of our forefathers has proved again and again to be folly; their humanity, bestiality; their ideas of honour and justice things to weep over. To think as so many, perhaps unconsciously, think: ' War must be justifiable if the united opinion of mankind has accepted it for all these centuries ', is to forget the abominations which mankind, after 'all these centuries', has only just managed to reject. War has not lasted so very much longer than slavery and the rack and the burning of heretics.

I invite the Church, which has so recently lost its faith in the rack and the stake, to make an effort to lose its faith in war.

The Church, we may assume, regards murder as a sin against God. In most cases murder is an attempt by an individual to end a situation which can only be ended by the removal of some other individual. The sole reason for the murder is that the death of this other will preserve or increase the wealth, happiness or safety of the murderer.

War is an attempt by an organized group of people to end a situation which can only be ended by the removal of some other group's opposition. This opposition can only be removed by the killing of large numbers of the opposing group. The sole reason for the killing is that the deaths of these people will (it is assumed) preserve or increase the wealth, happiness or safety of the group to which the killers belong.

The motive for war, then, would seem to be identical with the motive for murder, the result to be the same, but multiplied a million times. It would seem that, if it be wrong to kill one other man who gets in the way, it must be wrong to kill a million other men who get in the way. Yet the

Church says that it is not wrong. Let us ask somebody why.

M. Well?

C. (*but whether the Archbishop of Canterbury or his humblest Curate ; whether Canon, Clergyman or Christian, I cannot say*) : To begin with, you are entirely ignoring the vital distinction between aggressive and defensive war.

M. Does the Church make this distinction?

C. Of course. Just as it makes the obvious distinction between the attempt to murder and the attempt to resist murder. If a man makes an unprovoked assault upon me with a knife, I am entitled to resist, and if I can only save myself by taking his life, both the Church and the Law will absolve me.

M. But they will not absolve the would-be murderer?

C. Of course not.

M. What you mean, then, is that if a country wantonly attacks another country, the Church will absolve the defending country of the lives it takes in its own defence?

C. Of course.

M. And denounce and condemn the attacking country?

C. Precisely.

M. Has the Church of England ever denounced England for this reason?

C. I am proud to think that it has never had occasion to.

M. Even the Boer War was a war of defence? An attempt to resist invasion—murder—attack—defeat—what?

C. I think it would be right to say that the Christian conscience was a little disturbed by some of the—er—undercurrents of the Boer War, but——

M. But the Church didn't actually denounce England?

C. No.

M. Has any national Church ever denounced its own country?

C. That I cannot say.

M. It would almost seem, wouldn't it, that the 'vital distinction' is not between aggression and defence, but between one's own country and the enemy's country?

C. There is nothing to prevent a Christian being a patriot.

M. The point is, which comes first in his mind? Patriotism or Christianity? Which gives way to the other?

C. Nothing can come before a man's duty to his God. But just as a devoted son will, without intention, judge his mother over-leniently, so a

Christian may, without intention, judge his country over-leniently.

M. The Church of Rome is not a national Church?

C. No.

M. The Pope has no national prejudices?

C. I imagine not.

M. Since the last war cannot have been a completely defensive war on the part of all nations, one nation at least must have merited the condemnation of Christ. Did the Vicar of Christ condemn that nation? Did he threaten to excommunicate all Catholics who fought for that nation? Did he denounce them as murderers?

C. As head of an international Church the Pope is in a difficult position. I imagine that it is his endeavour to avoid judging between nations.

M. Then since the Head of an international Church avoids judging between nations, and the Head of a national Church avoids condemning his own nation, it would seem that the vital distinction between the aggressive nation and the defensive nation is not only ignored by me, but also by the Churches.

C. I cannot admit that.

M. Very well, then. Let us assume that England, alone among nations, only fights defensive wars.

C. I cannot admit anything else.

M. And that in fighting them she takes human lives in great numbers.

C. It is inevitable.

M. Generally speaking, the Church holds the view that human life is sacred ?

C. Yes.

M. So sacred that a man may not even take his own life to end intolerable pain or unhappiness ?

C. The Church condemns suicide, yes.

M. Because each of us is in God's hands, and it is for Him to decide when death shall come ?

C. Yes.

M. Then either war takes the decision out of God's hands, in which case it is a sin, or war is ordained by God, and we are not responsible for it. Which ?

C. Of course we are responsible ; but whatever the Churches have said or not said in the past, I am convinced that God Himself, who knows all hearts, will distinguish between those who deliberately make war, and those who merely repel it.

M. ' Repelling war ' means, does it not, accepting the ordeal of battle ? Even if this entails the loss of a million sacred lives, it is not a sin ?

C. The mere fact of causing the death of a human being is not necessarily a sin. If it were so, then the execution of a murderer would be a sin.

M. Roughly speaking, you would compare murder and capital punishment with (say) the invasion of a country and the repulsion of the invaders?

C. Roughly, yes.

M. But is not the sole moral justification of capital punishment the fact that it *saves* lives? Is not the argument that, if there were no executions, there would be many more murders? And is not this the only possible argument for the Church to admit?

C. Yes, I think perhaps that is true.

M. On the other hand, the acceptance of the ordeal of battle is certain to bring about thousands of deaths which would not otherwise have occurred. What is the moral justification of that?

C. Are you really suggesting that England should totally ignore a declaration of war, and make no defence whatever to an armed invasion?

M. I am suggesting that you should give me the views of a Christian Church, not of the Navy League.

C. To any Christian the idea of accepting passively such a wrong is intolerable.

M. In the sense that who can't suffer what?

C. Do you really mean that you are prepared for a German army to march through the streets of London, for Germany to dictate whatever humiliating terms she pleases, to exact indemnities, to make unlawful annexations, to——

M. Please, *please* pull yourself together! I am not prepared for, in the sense of being happily acquiescent in, any of these things. In fact, I should hate them. It would be easy to feel intensely humiliated by them. But then it is easy for an author to feel intensely humiliated whenever his play is rejected or his novel is a failure. It is easy for a clerk to hate being dictated to by a bullying employer. Even a clergyman can feel humiliated by the emptiness of his church or the reproof of his Bishop. But we don't go killing people in order to relieve, or prevent, our humiliation. Whence do you get this extraordinary Christian idea that, though Man must suffer all things rather than do wrong, a nation can do all the wrong it likes rather than suffer anything?

C. I think you exaggerate.

M. For Heaven's sake, and the Church's sake, don't let me exaggerate. Let us get at the truth. If in 1940 a re-armed Germany, thirsting for revenge, declared war on England, you would approve of England taking up arms in defence?

C. She would be reluctantly forced to.

M. Which being so, you would approve?

C. Yes.

M. And approve of her killing as many Germans—men, women and children—as possible?

C. Certainly not women and children.

M. Please be honest about it. You know that aeroplanes are used in war; you know that a nation which accepts the ordeal of battle uses all the weapons of war; you know that, if aeroplanes are used, women and children are killed. You would approve, then, of your country killing as many Germans—men, women and children—as was necessary to break the enemy's spirit and end the war?

C. As many (alas!) as were inevitable, but no more, I hope, than were necessary.

M. And you would not call that sort of killing murder?

C. No.

M. Suppose that the war became general, new alliances were formed, and in the end our only hope of victory lay in the armed support of Russia. Suppose that Russia made it a condition of her support that the English people should renounce God—as, officially, she herself has done. Would the Church approve of a solemn renunciation of God by the Government on behalf of the people?

C. Are you deliberately trying to insult the Church?

M. Put it that I am deliberately trying to see if the Church *can* be insulted. Well?

C. The answer is No.

M. Suppose it were Turkey, and it was thought that the Turks would fight better if officially we became Mohammedans, and all shared the same religious enthusiasms? Would you approve?

C. The answer is No.

M. We could always change back afterwards.

C. And add a lie to the sin on our soul?

M. But you don't object to lies, surely? You never have objected in any other war. Or did you really think that all the bulletins from the Front were true?

C. I admit sadly that in war——

M. May I take it as definite, then, that the Church would not approve of England renouncing Christianity or embracing Mohammedanism, even if these were the only ways of avoiding defeat?

C. You may.

M. And that, rather than consent to a recantation of your faith, you would be prepared for a German army to march through London, for Germany to dictate whatever humiliating terms she pleased, to exact indemnities, to make unlawful annexations, to——

C. Certainly.

M. You see what I am looking for, don't you? The point where Christianity ends and Patriotism begins. Let us go on looking for it. Suppose that in 1920 an inspired statesman had foreseen this war of 1940; had been convinced that it would be a war of attrition; and had realized that England's only hope lay in a *maximum* increase of population. Suppose that the Government had passed a law requiring immediate marriage and begetting of children from all adult males; and, since this would leave two million females still unmarried, had called for two million volunteers to commit adultery. Would the Church have approved?

C. Does that require an answer?

M. Most urgently. The Church has already said that it approves of murder on behalf of the State; I want to know if it approves of adultery.

C. I have already said that I do not call it murder.

M. But then you needn't call it adultery. You could call it ' Enlisting as a Temporary Husband '. *Pro patria* . . . Well?

C. You know perfectly well what the answer is.

M. I assure you on my honour that I do not.

(And so, not knowing what the answer is, I shall not attempt to give it.)

But I hope that it was beginning to be clear whither the argument was leading us. It is difficult to see how a Church, which approves deliberate killing so long as it is *pro patria*, can afford to be horrified at deliberate adultery which is also *pro patria*. It is equally difficult, at the moment, to imagine the Church of England giving its blessing to adultery, however patriotically conceived. If we try to reconcile these two difficulties, we shall come inevitably to the conclusion that the killing is approved because it is the conventional way of exhibiting patriotism, and that the adultery is only condemned because there is no tradition of patriotism behind it. For, logically, if a man puts his country before his God, he is bound to add acceptance of adultery and recantation to his acceptance of killing ; and equally bound to reject all three if he puts his God first.

3

To a famous Churchman of an earlier day are attributed these words :

> 'Had I but served my God with half the zeal
> I served my King, he would not in mine age
> Have left me naked to mine enemies.'

It is strange that he should have thought this. The Church to-day seems pledged to the belief that service to King and Country, whatever unlovely shape it takes, is, in some odd but inevitable way, service to God. A creed so startling demands Divine authority, and Divine authority is found in two texts from the Gospels, recording the words of Christ. It is not suggested, of course, that Christ actually had the Great War in his mind when He spoke the words, but the words do show, as a Christian gentleman assured the world the other day, ' what Christ thought of Pacifists '.

1. *' When a strong man armed keepeth his palace, his goods are in peace '* (Luke xi. 21).

The Christian apologist for war stops there, conveniently, hoping that the irreligious Pacifist doesn't read his Bible. For the next verse says: ' But when a stronger than he shall come upon him, and overcome him, he taketh from him all his armour wherein he trusted, and divideth his spoils '; which seems to show what Christ thought of Militarists. For the occasion of these words was the casting-out of a devil; and, as will be remembered, some of the people said : ' He casteth out devils through Beelzebub the chief of the devils.' Whereupon Christ explained that Satan could not cast out Satan, and that devils could only be cast out by somebody stronger than themselves. So, in the parable which follows, the ' strong man armed ' is Beelzebub, and the ' stronger than he ', who takes from him ' *all his armour wherein he trusted* ', is God. It is not altogether out of keeping with Christ's character as we know it to suppose that armour did not make any very powerful appeal to Him ; and it is not out of keeping with the situation to assume that the miracle of healing which He had just performed was not meant as a preliminary to the use of mustard-gas.

However, Christ also said this :

2. '*Render unto Caesar the things which are Caesar's ; and unto God the things that are God's*' (Matthew xxii. 21).

This much-quoted text is generally held to justify the partition of one's soul. One cannot serve God and Mammon, no ; but Caesar and God, yes, even when they seem to beckon in opposite directions.

Now the interesting thing about these words of Christ's is that they were not said to the Romans but to the Jews ; and the Jews were a conquered race. Their conquerors were ruling in Jerusalem : just as (in the apprehension of the Patriot) the Germans will be ruling in London, if we don't get some more aeroplanes. Now if we can imagine Christ coming to London at some future time when England has surrendered to Germany, and if we can imagine Mr. Winston Churchill asking Him if we ought meekly to pay the indemnity exacted of us, and if Christ replied : ' Render unto Hitler the things which are Hitler's ; and unto God the things that are God's ', we can see that Mr. Churchill's patriotic spirit would not be greatly encouraged. What he would want to be told would be that the secret poison-gas factory at Gleneagles and the undisclosed treaty with Switzerland justified an armed repudiation of the terms of Peace. And he has been told precisely the opposite.

For if Christ's answer is more than an escape from a dilemma, it is saying clearly: 'What matter if we are a conquered race, so long as we continue to serve God?'

It is doubtful, then, whether either of these texts really gives that Divine authority to war which the Christian must surely ask. Possibly the authority is given in some other words of Christ's which I have overlooked. (For instance: 'If thy right hand offend thee, cut it off' may have referred to the fact that Germany is on the right hand of France, looking towards the North Pole.) But, even if I found the words, I should still be uncertain as to what interpretation I was meant to put on them. For there seem to be two possible theories which could be advanced in justification of Christianity's approval of war, and I do not know which of them my text should favour.

THEORY A: *Obedience to the State is God's first law, and takes precedence of all other laws which He has made.*

THEORY B: *What is called the Safety of the State is of such importance in God's sight that He holds a nation to be justified in using any means to achieve it.*

The difference between these two theories will be clear if we consider certain practical, though extravagant, applications of them.

Under Theory A:

A Government (either from sheer wilfulness or for the most patriotic reasons) orders, and obtains, a general indulgence in incest.
Then:
1. The members of the Government have to answer to God for their sin.
2. The people are absolved. (Unless they refuse to commit incest: in which case they have broken God's first law.)

Under Theory B:

A Government orders a general indulgence in incest.
Then:
1. If the order is made from sheer wilfulness, not only the members of the Government but also the people are answerable to God for their sin.
2. If the order is necessary for the salvation

of the State, nobody is answerable to God, since His sanction is already assured.

[*Note*.—As this still leaves it uncertain whether the responsibility of justifying the order is the Government's or the individual's, we seem to want two Sub-theories. Under Sub-theory α the individual may accept the Government's plea of necessity, and claim absolution. Under Sub-theory β the individual must refer the plea of necessity to his own conscience.]

But even when we have decided for which of these theories we have found textual justification, there is still the difficulty of deciding at what point in the growth of a community the text begins to apply. It seems certain that, if two people declare war on each other, and throw bombs into each other's houses, the death or mutilation of their families has not the Divine sanction. Is the sanction, then, given to any two *groups* of people : say to twelve people on a desert island divided into two groups of six ? If not, is it only given to communities ; or to communities which have the standing of a nation ? And is the decision when a group becomes a community, or a community becomes a nation, in the hands of God or in the hands of the latest Peace Conference ? Does God wait for Lloyd George and Clemenceau to tell Him which new groups of people are to be allowed a free hand with the Ten Commandments, and are their names then duly registered in Heaven on a special White List?

Much of all this may sound frivolous or far-fetched; but I shall not mind, even if it is called ' facetious ' and ' not in the best of taste '. It is designed to make people think again, *and from the beginning*, about war. Modern war means (among other things in this year of grace), quite definitely and without any mental escape, choking and poisoning and torturing to death thousands, probably hundreds of thousands, of women and children. Whether you are Christian or Jew, atheist or agnostic, you have got to fit acceptance of this into your philosophy of life. It is not enough to say : ' What else can nations do ? ' It is not enough, nor is it even true, to say : ' It has always been so.' Here is the fact now, and you have got to justify to yourself your acceptance of it ; and the justification has got to be based on such ultimate truths as will always be sacred to you.

CHAPTER IX

TEN MILLION—AND FORTY

THE previous chapter must be regarded as an interlude. Doubtless it was omitted by the many who feel that religion is only meant for women, children and one's own last moments. But since the call to arms comes through the voices of ' King and Country ', and since the King is not only Emperor of India but also Defender of the Faith, one had some justification for asking what the Faith was which we were all (presumably) defending. In this chapter, which is concerned with politicians, Christianity will find no sort of a loophole through which to intrude.

It has been said that, if there were a law, made and enforced by all nations, that on the outbreak of war the Prime Minister and Foreign Secretary of the countries concerned were immediately hanged, then there would be no more war in Europe. This was said in the days when Parliamentary Government was more fashionable than it is now. But let us adapt and amplify the saying for modern use. Let us suppose that certain people were assured that, if ever there were another war in Europe on the scale of the last war, they themselves would be the first victims of it. What would happen?

First of all, we must select our victims, and for this purpose we will limit ourselves to the four Great Powers most likely to be concerned: England, France, Germany and Italy. From Italy we need only choose Mussolini; from Germany, Hitler, Goering and Goebbels. England being a democratic country, offers us a wider choice. I suggest the following:

Ramsay MacDonald, Baldwin, Simon. One unnamed Cabinet Minister, chosen by lot on the day that war is declared. The Ministers responsible for the fighting services. Winston Churchill. Two unnamed Generals, two unnamed Admirals and two unnamed directors of armament firms, also chosen by lot. Lords Beaverbrook and Rothermere, and the Editors of *The Times* and the *Morning Post*.

France's politics being more fluid, it will be unprofitable to give names in advance, so let us decide merely that she furnishes a corresponding equality of victims with England.

Now here are forty people who are all going to die as a preliminary to the next war. Are the chances of another war lessened?

I can hear the Elder Statesman saying that ' since

the premiss is entirely outside the sphere of practical politics, any conclusion drawn from it is purely theoretical and therefore valueless'. Theoretical, yes: but not valueless. On the contrary, it will be of the utmost value in helping us to appreciate the meaning of the war-convention. I beg my readers, therefore, to pretend, by a supreme exercise of the imagination, that my premiss is in actual practice. I know that many people find it difficult to imagine the obviously impossible. It is, of course, impossible that on the outbreak of a war these forty important persons should die, as for the purpose of this chapter they ought to die: that is, as men die in war: some with merciful quickness, some in slow agony. But it is not wholly impossible that they should be genuinely intent on peace; should believe that the certainty of their own deaths would keep them from ensuing war unnecessarily; should take a solemn oath to commit suicide on the outbreak of war; and (most unlikely supposition of all, but, I suppose, just conceivable) should keep their oath if war broke out. This being so, our premiss should be within the imagination of all of us. Assume, then, with confidence that these forty leaders are to be the first victims of the next war, and ask yourself whether the peace of Europe is the more assured.

Can there be any doubt? My own conviction

is that, so long as these forty people exercised their present influence, any war between their countries would be 'entirely outside the sphere of practical politics'.

Now if this were indeed so : if it were the truth that these forty leaders would never in any circumstances condemn themselves to death : then the war convention is definitely exposed as the ridiculous imposture which so many of us believe it to be. For the convention is that war is 'a biological necessity' : an 'inevitable outlet of human nature'; that it is 'the extreme expression of Patriotism' (than which there is no higher religion); that it 'stamps the mark of nobility upon nations'; that it provides opportunities (10,000,000 in the last war) of a 'pleasant and fitting' death ; in short, that it is ultimately the only way and the inevitable way and the noblest way of settling disputes between nations. But these forty people cannot seriously hold any of these beliefs if they are deterred from giving expression to them by such a trifle as their own forty pleasant and fitting deaths among ten million others. War is inevitable ? Then they will not be able to avert it. War is human nature ? But they also are subject to human impulses. War is the extreme expression of Patriotism ? Well, who so patriotic as they ? And so, if they showed (as I think they would show) that they *could* avert even the threat of war ; if they affirmed (as I think they would affirm) that Patriotism and Peace were allies, not enemies ; if, for the preservation of their own lives, they prevented (as I think they would prevent) ten million other people from dying gloriously for their country ; then they would have given the lie to all the traditional theories which they have propagated about war. For war could not be less natural, less inevitable, less noble with 10,000,040 lives at stake than it was with 10,000,000.

To believe, then, that there would be no more war if the makers of it were always the first victims is to surrender all faith in war. It is to proclaim oneself as convinced a Pacifist as the writer of this book. If our rulers could keep us from war (without dimming the sacred lamp of Patriotism) when their own lives were at hazard, they can keep us from war now ; they can always keep us from war ; and the Millennium is within our reach.

But the Patriot is not as convinced a Pacifist as the author of this book. He declares, indignantly, therefore, that not for one moment does he believe that there would be no more war if these great men were to be the first victims. It would make (he swears) no difference at all. Mr. Winston Churchill (he says, doffing his hat) would be as thrilled by an ultimatum as ever ; the patriotism of Pertinax would burn no less fiercely ;

Goering and Mussolini would continue to extol the glories of dying for their country; war lords and armament kings and newspaper proprietors would prepare for battle as ardently as before. In fact, the world would go on just as it goes on now, and the next Armageddon would be as near or as remote.

So he would say. So he must swear, if he is not to forswear himself.

But—*is he sure?*

Let him think . . . and think . . . and think again. And if it will help him to think truly, let him, just before he begins, imagine one more victim added to the forty. Himself.

Now then. Forty-one are to die with the first shot of war, and the shadow of war lies over Europe. What are the forty-one doing? What are they thinking?

Here are Mussolini and Hitler and Simon and the Frenchman in conference together. Does war seem quite so glorious to Mussolini? Does Germany's destiny lie so certainly on the battlefield? Is a 'preventive war' so necessary to France? (So immediately necessary? Cannot we live a few more years?) Is England's honour bound up so intimately with the mutilation of women and children? Let us be reasonable. Let us talk it over calmly. Are we always to be slaves to the war-convention? Surely we are intelligent men.

Brave men, certainly, and patriots ; ready enough to sacrifice our lives. But for what shall we be dying ? To save others—when by our very deaths we condemn ten million to death ? For civilization ? By dying, we bring civilization down in ruins. . . .

The war cloud is growing bigger. Somebody has insulted somebody else's flag. Somebody's prestige is threatened. Somebody's security may be in danger some day. Here are our editors and newspaper proprietors preparing their leading articles.

How aggressive are they, how patriotic, how swashbuckling ? Does it make no difference to Lords Beaverbrook and Rothermere that when war comes, they will take no safe but active part in it ? Governments will fall, but not through their public-spirited endeavours. Governments will rise, but not with their patronage. They will be dead. . . .

Here is Mr. Winston Churchill. Indeed, no one so fearless as he, nor so ready to die heroically for England. But he would like to live heroically first. If war comes, he would like to lead a forlorn hope somewhere . . . one that would leave him free to lead another forlorn hope afterwards, somewhere else. He would die gloriously for anybody, or anything ; even ingloriously (and by the conditions of his oath he is hanging himself privately). But—ought he? Death has no terrors, but it has disabilities. Dead men are never Prime Ministers, for instance. Ought he not to sacrifice his inclination to war to his duty to his country? He goes to prepare his great 'crisis' speech at Twickenham. How bellicose is it?

And here is our Patriot. What is he thinking? In the early summer of 1914 I heard him saying (himself well past the military age): 'England is getting slack. What she needs is a war to wake her up.' Well, she had it. But does he say that now? Does the Pacifist ideal of a world without war seem so contemptible to him? When he opens his *Morning Post* is he delighted to see that the Government and the Editor are 'taking a firm line'? Does he look at the little bottle of cyanide in the medicine cupboard, and say proudly to himself: 'In a few days now I shall be drinking that'? How militant is he? . . .

So I ask him again: Is he *certain* that the assurance of their own deaths would make no difference to the war-minded? Is he certain that not by one hour would an ultimatum be delayed, that not by one provocative word the less would deadlock be averted? For if it only made that much difference, then all that the Patriot has said about war is proved false.

TEN MILLION—AND FORTY

2

It should be clear by this time that my theme all through this book has been that the obstacle to Peace is man's subservience to the war *convention*. Let us consider some other convention and see how completely it acts as a substitute for thought. It is March as I write this chapter, and my newspaper gives me what I want.

Two universities compete every year in a boat-race. 'Blues' are awarded—that is, the crews are definitely chosen—about six weeks before the race. For six weeks the names of these eighteen men are printed every morning in the newspaper. Every morning for six weeks the record of their weights is also printed. Sometimes one of them has gone up by as much as ¼ lb. in the last twenty-four hours, and it may be that in the next twenty-four hours his weight will have receded by ½ lb. England is kept in touch with these movements.

Now when a University crew is chosen, it is interesting (for those interested in rowing or the University) to be told that a man in a certain position in the middle of the boat is a fine big fellow of 14 stone ; but the additional facts that on some mornings he is 14·1, and on others 13·13, do not help us to visualize him any more clearly. Indeed, we could almost have guessed that a man who weighs 14 stone on one morning will weigh

14·1 on some other morning. No doubt weight is important to an oarsman. But it is equally important to a Rugby forward—and newspaper readers are as interested in football as in rowing. Yet, when the English Rugby team is chosen, we are not given a daily chart of their weights. Indeed, we are not told their weights at all. Nor are their names announced day after day until the match is played.

It would appear, then, that the treatment of the University Boat Race in the papers is the result of convention, not of original thought. No editor says to himself: 'Good Heavens! Tomkins was 12·6½ yesterday, and he is 12·7 to-day! This is news. We must let our readers in on this.' Nor, on the other hand, does he say to himself: 'This is the twenty-eighth consecutive day on which we have printed the names of these people. Surely if anybody is interested in the crew he will have learnt their names by now, and in any case he'll see them again to-morrow. Couldn't we save an inch of space to-day, and get in that paragraph about the baby who swallowed the safety-pin, or the arrival at Geneva of the new deputy for Peru?' He does not say these things, because he gives the matter no conscious thought at all. His mind accepts automatically the convention that any mention of the crews is followed by their names and weights.

TEN MILLION—AND FORTY

With just the same automatic acceptance of convention the politician assumes that an 'international deadlock' is followed by 'war'. The fact that 'war' once meant a thousand a side with bows and arrows, and now means ten million a side with bombs and poison-gas, has no message for him. He is not visualizing war. He is simply letting international politics take their course in the conventional way. When a consulting specialist orders his client a long sea voyage, he is not visualizing a long sea voyage. He neither knows nor cares whether the sufferer can afford a long sea voyage. All he is doing is to obey his automatic reflex to a particular condition of the body he is examining. To such-and-such a condition one says 'Long sea voyage'. In the same way the politician's automatic reflex to a certain condition of the body politic is to say 'War'—which is the conventional way of ending that condition.

When, therefore, I suggest that politicians would not say 'War' if they themselves were the first victims of it, I am not doubting their courage, nor their appetite for self-sacrifice. I am doubting their imagination. In most people's imagination the gulf between their own death and somebody else's is almost unbridgeable. For the average person we could construct a Table of Comparative Deaths, which might go like this:

10,000,000 deaths from famine in China
 = (in horror) 100,000 deaths from earthquake in Sicily
 = (in horror) 1,000 deaths from influenza in Brighton
 = (in horror) 10 deaths from typhoid in one's own village
 = (in horror) 1 sudden death of a friend.
Sudden death of 1,000 friends = (in horror) DEATH OF ONESELF.

Assuming such a table to be somewhere near the truth, we can see how much more hopeful the cause of Peace would be if war were realized in terms of one's own death rather than in terms of the death of strangers. Actually politicians hardly realize war in terms of death at all. No doubt fighting a war means killing people. No doubt reading a book means turning the pages. But nobody thinks of reading as finger-exercise. If the war-maker could be made to think of war as meaning inevitably his own death, then he might be able to think of war as meaning ten million deaths.

For, at present, his attitude to the ten million is a strange mixture of cynicism and sentimentality. In Mr. Beverley Nichols' book *Cry Havoc* there is a chapter entitled 'Skunk *v.* Bengal Lancer', which records an actual dialogue between

'an intelligent man of war' (Yeats Brown) and 'an intelligent man of peace' (Robert Mennel). One of the questions which the intelligent man of war asks his opponent is this:
"Why do you consider it so important that people should not lose their lives? . . . A man's got to die some time, why should he not die by being shot as by any other means?' And then, inevitably but hardly intelligently, he adds: 'Surely to be shot is as good as dying of cancer or fatty degeneration of the heart.'

I need not point out again that death in war is not necessarily caused by a rifle bullet through the centre of the forehead; nor death in peace by cancer. But if the intelligent man of war wishes to know why death is taken so seriously by so many people, I will tell him.

The reason is this: Death is final. When one has said that, one has said everything. Death is the worst thing that can happen, because it is the last thing that can happen. Whatever other disaster should come to him, a man still has the alternative of death in front of him if he wishes it. But when death comes to him, he cannot choose the alternative of some other disaster. Whatever you do to a man, if you leave him his life, you leave him not only life, but, if he prefers it, death. If you take away his life you leave him, in this world, nothing.

The proud and intelligent man of war may deny this indignantly. He says that he would far, far sooner see his son dead than in prison for fraud. But I will remind him, first: that imprisonment for fraud (if just) is not 'a disaster which comes', but something which is deliberately invited; and secondly: that it is not a question of what *he* would prefer, but what his son would prefer. By all means let the proud and intelligent man of war court death, embrace death, expire beautifully in the arms of death. But he has no right whatever to prescribe death for others. Even if death were no more 'important' than a cold in the head or tapioca pudding, I should still feel strongly that he had no right to insist on colds in the head and tapioca pudding for everybody.

About actual death in war, then (or, as he prefers to call it, 'being shot'), our militarist is charmingly callous. But now hear him on the real horror of extinction. In support of his contention that frontier disputes are inevitable, and must inevitably be solved by war, he says:

'Supposing you were like a Hungarian I have heard of, who has had the Rumanian frontier ruled right through his estate, so that while his house is still in Hungary his family mausoleum is in Rumania. What would you say if you couldn't put flowers on your mother's grave without asking permission of a foreign sentry?'

It is almost inconceivable that a man's mind should work like this. As a result of the last war, a million English wives and mothers cannot put flowers on their loved ones' graves without going into a foreign country to do it. What does our militarist suppose that they say? 'Let's have another war'? If it is so desperately important to be able to put flowers on graves without crossing a frontier (even though death itself is unimportant), obviously a war is the one means of death which should be avoided. For unless each country fights within its own boundaries (which hardly seems practicable), 50 per cent. of the dead will die on foreign soil.

In 1922, when we were so nearly at war again with Turkey, *Punch* made a noble and patriotic appeal to the country to 'defend the sanctity of our graves in Gallipoli'; which it proposed to do by providing material for yet more graves in Gallipoli. Apparently it is only the grave of the dead man which is sacred to the sentimental militarist. Life itself is not sacred.

3

And so, in order to bring it home to the sentimental militarist and the patriotic politician how very sacred life really is, I will ask one more hypothetical question. The Patriot has said often enough that, if the Polish Corridor were threatened, it would be the duty of England to take up arms. Well, suppose that the Polish Corridor were threatened; suppose that he were assured that, if he allowed himself to be tortured to death through to-morrow and the next day, the Polish Corridor would be kept securely in being; would he consent?

There are three answers which he may give.

1. *Certainly.* (Death being unimportant.)

If that be an honest answer, I can only bow my head in humble admiration.

2. *Certainly not.*

Yet, if his words drive England into war, he is condemning thousands of Englishmen to a death which he refuses for himself.

3. *It isn't a fair question.*

Ah! How often have we heard that answer!

And what does it mean? It means that he has never thought of war as equivalent to anything so important as his own death. He may say that he would be perfectly willing to take his chance: of a quick death, or a slow death, or safety: and that he is asking no more of anybody else. Of any individual, no. But he is definitely demanding agonizing deaths from thousands, and the fact that he cannot give their names in advance does not seem to make his responsibility any the less. I say that the question is a simple one and a fair one. He is demanding the sacrifice of thousands

TEN MILLION—AND FORTY

of lives for the maintenance of the Polish Corridor. Will he, here and now, sacrifice his own?

Well—will he?

I don't suppose he has ever thought about it. To the Patriot the Polish Corridor is simply 'the sort of thing one goes to war about'. *It always has been.*

I wonder how many people share my conviction that, if a few Patriots were hanged, it never would be again.

CHAPTER X

'NOT TOO PACIFIST, I HOPE'

I

IN the interval between writing the last chapter and beginning this one I was playing golf with a young woman, and it happened that we were held up for a little on the eleventh tee. As we sat there, admiring the view, she said :
'Are you very busy just now ? '
'I am rather,' I said.
'What is it, a play ? '
'No, a book.'
'Oh, a novel ? '
'Well, no. . . . It's a book about war.'
There was a short silence, and then she said :
'You mean *against* war ? '
'Yes.'
'Not *too* pacifist, I hope,' she smiled.

Three days after Armistice Day last year there was a letter from a woman in the *Morning Post*. It said :
'I notice that he—[Mr. Rudyard Kipling, no

'NOT TOO PACIFIST, I HOPE'

less]—lays a great deal of the blame for disarmament and the unpreparedness for war at the door of the women. Does not the real blame lie at the door of our leading public men, who have for a period of years headed an intensive peace propaganda?'

Obviously, in the opinion of this correspondent, 'heading an intensive peace propaganda' is being 'too pacifist'.

One may call oneself a peace-lover, but one must be careful not to love it too much.

With every page that I write, with every day that passes, I become more and more convinced that when we talk about 'Peace' and 'War', we are thinking in words which have completely changed their value. Peace for many people still means something priggish and cowardly; War still means something manly and self-sacrificing. If you are 'too pacifist', then you don't really love your country, you are unpleasantly anxious to 'save your own skin', and probably you think that football is a very rough game.

Now it is an interesting, if obvious, fact that nobody who talks bravely about war has ever been killed in war. Every word which has been uttered about the pleasantness of dying for one's country, every airy reference to death as a thing of minor importance, has been spoken by somebody who has not experienced death, but who could experience it at any moment if he really wished. Of the men and women who talk so gallantly to-day about war, 90 per cent. have never encountered it, even though some of them may have worn uniforms. The remaining 10 per cent. (if, indeed, it be as many as 10 per cent.) survived the War. To be gallant and dashing and manly about an adventure which one has never had; to be brave about a danger which one has passed; this is not a courage whose badge the Pacifist is morbidly desirous of winning. When the young men of Oxford resolved never again to fight for 'King and Country', a certain noble member of the Government called them in his graceful way 'yellow-bellied'. Whether he considered that those who opposed the motion were red-bellied (or possibly, like himself, blue-bellied) was not made public. But if he had been able to spare the time for thought, or had had anything to think with, he would have realized that it is not a habit of the young to be anxious about the morrow; and that, in regard to a danger which may or may not materialize some years hence, it is quite impossible to be either brave or cowardly.

We may agree, then, I think, that Pacifists are not necessarily cowards, nor Militarists brave. Dare we go farther and suggest that war is not necessarily manly, nor peace effeminate?

Let us consider the suggestion by meeting our

'NOT TOO PACIFIST, I HOPE'

patriotic young women on their own ground : or what used to be their own ground : the domestic hearth.

Every cook nowadays has her 'rights'. Every young married woman has her 'rights'. From time to time what they think of as their rights will not be in accord. Suppose that when the rights of Cook and Mistress clash (on the point, say, of hot dinner on Sunday) war inevitably follows. China and cutlery is thrown, in a mild way at first, but soon more fiercely. Cook hurries from the house and returns with her male relations. Mistress drags her husband from his study, and telephones urgently for her brothers. The battle is then left to the men. There is a fierce set-to all over the house, the weapons of war being limited, by agreement, to fists, sticks and crockery. ... By evening peace is restored—or rather, dictated. Cook has won, and there are to be no hot dinners at all, not even on a weekday. Or Mistress has won, and Cook has no more evenings out, and pays for all the damage.

Now if the husband objects to living in a house like this, is anybody going to call him unmanly ? Is it unmanly to think that this method of existence is all wrong and utterly silly ? I don't mean just wrong and silly in our present ordered state, which gives us policemen and law-courts to meet these emergencies. I mean that, even in a community which lacked policemen, a sensitive, imaginative, intelligent man would feel that life lived like this was intolerable ; that it ought not to be beyond human powers to evolve something more dignified ; and that it was his duty to persuade his fellows to combine with him in search of that dignity. If he felt this, he could hardly be dismissed contemptuously as an effeminate creature who shirked being hit over the head with an umbrella.

In the last war ten million people were killed, and at least another ten million permanently affected, physically or mentally. If the manly Patriot contemplates this fact with an increased sense of virility, let him remember that this was not all that happened. Even had nobody been killed in the last war, the thought of its recurrence would still be intolerable to the sensitive and the intelligent. If a country is going to collect £7,000,000,000 from its people ; if it is going to take three million men away from their ordinary occupation for four years ; then it is possible to feel (without being unmanly) that there are more worthy ways of spending the time and money and employing the men than in sheer destruction. It is possible to feel that, sixteen years after the expenditure of that time and that money, one's country should have gained, rather than lost, in happiness, in dignity, and in beauty.

'NOT TOO PACIFIST, I HOPE'

2

Peace means freedom from war, not freedom from struggle. Getting up at six o'clock in the morning to earn a living is peace; hewing coal a mile beneath the surface of the earth is peace; climbing Everest, breaking a collar-bone at football, taking a boat single-handed across the Atlantic, fighting an outbreak of typhoid, flying an aeroplane to Australia, writing a hundred-thousand word book and then tearing it up and writing it again—all these things are forms of peace. In the days when the Latin tags were written, with which the up-to-date Patriot reassures himself, most of the hard work of the world was performed by living slaves and most of the sport provided by dying ones. Peaceful exploration was impossible, and mountains and sea were unknown as playgrounds. It is not a matter for surprise that an active young Roman should have welcomed war as something which offered a little excitement at first hand, and gave him, at last, an opportunity of showing his strength, his skill and his courage.

The modern Englishman can show his courage every day by crossing Piccadilly Circus. He can ride in the Grand National, fly an aeroplane, compete at Brooklands, dive off Brighton pier, challenge Petersen to fight, stand up to Larwood's bowling, and join a blood-transfusion society. There is no reason whatever why the intolerable nuisance of war should spread itself over Europe for four years in order that an Englishman should be able to exhibit his manliness, and an Englishwoman be able to experience vicariously that grand, heroic feeling.

I have called war an intolerable nuisance. It is interesting, if hardly surprising, to find that, just as the war-makers, who condemn millions to death, are the very people who will not themselves be facing death, so are they just the people to whom war is not an interruption of their ordinary life. Who are the men responsible for war? Obviously not poets and painters, and butchers and bakers, and farmers and doctors and candlestick makers. However we divide the credit, we can say that those responsible for it must necessarily be found among politicians, soldiers and sailors of high rank, financiers, armament kings, and newspaper proprietors, editors and leader-writers. And what happens when war breaks out? All these people merely intensify their previous activities. Not one of them interrupts his work at his country's call. Indeed, to nearly all of them an outbreak of war is just an opportunity of greater fame, greater self-expression and greater rewards. In the last chapter I said that, if they were all to be hanged on the declaration of war, war would never be declared. I am inclined to think that it would be enough if they were all put to safe but homely jobs in the Sanitary Squad.

So, if the virile Patriot still feels that a violent hatred of war can only come from the cowardly and the effeminate, let him think of war as four years' interruption of life (in a sanitary squad) and four years' waste of money at the rate of £7,000,000 a day; and he will understand what excellent other reasons there are for hating it. Let him then think of war in terms of Profiteers, Embusqués, Nepotism, Job-wangling, War Diaries, Propaganda, Rumours, Spy-mania, Honours Lists, Staff Appointments, Patriotic Songs, ' Combing Out ', White Feathers, Business as Usual, and Keeping the Home Fires Burning; Hatred and Malice and all Uncharitableness; and then Lies and Lies and still more Lies, and the apotheosis of all the Bottomleys, Kreugers and Staviskys of the world. That is modern war. Leave out the ten million dead soldiers; we can be brave and hearty about ' our gallant boys '—*dulce et decorum est pro patria mori*; but add a few hundred thousand mutilated women and a few hundred thousand starved children . . . and then reflect that this is only the beginning of it. This is only the comparatively short Four Years' War. There are still sixteen years of post-war virility to come.

Crushing taxation ; shackles on liberty from which we shall never again be free ; millions of unemployed in whom hope is almost dead ; a rising generation in whom hope was never born ; and Anarchy and Autocracy fighting a last desperate battle among the ruins. . . .

There was a short silence, and then she said :
'You mean you are *against* war ? '
'Yes.'
'Not *too* pacifist, I hope,' she smiled.

CHAPTER XI
HUMAN NATURE

I

MILITARISTS are accustomed to say that 'so long as human nature is what it is' we shall never be able to renounce war, and that 'only when we are all saints' will there be any hope of settling our differences by friendly agreement.

We need not be saints. It will be enough if we stop being criminal lunatics.

Thirty-five years ago Lord Kitchener, advancing up the Nile after the victory of Omdurman, reached a village called Fashoda. There he found a French Major, by name Marchand, who announced that he had taken possession of Fashoda in the name of his country. The news was cabled to Europe; the statesmen and the publicists and the editors got to work; and for a little while it seemed that they would be successful in arranging a war on the grand scale between England and France.

There was, however, no war. Possibly the

idea of war, even to politicians, seemed too comic. Possibly the thought of French sailors (who had never heard before of Fashoda) hurrying off to the North Sea and firing an 81-ton gun at an invisible battleship manned by English sailors who had also never heard before of Fashoda, when Fashoda was, in any case, only a fever-haunted village in the middle of an African swamp four thousand miles away—possibly the thought of this made them laugh. But if war had come: a war for a mosquito-ridden swamp, between a nation of realists and a nation of shopkeepers: would it have been true to say that, after all, it was only human nature?

This is not how human nature comes out. If Lord Kitchener, annoyed equally by the presence of the mosquitoes and the presence of the Major, had lost his temper and hit Marchand on the jaw; if Marchand had picked himself up and challenged Kitchener to a duel; even if English soldiers had got out of hand, and, being the stronger force, had chased the Frenchmen out of the village; well, then one might have excused them on the ground that men could not always control their impulses, particularly in a hot climate, and that, after all, one mustn't expect soldiers to be saints. Actually none of this happened. Kitchener and Marchand, as was not unnatural in a hot climate, had a drink together . . . and four thousand miles away their respective Prime Ministers wondered whether they could pretend that their countries were convulsed by such ungovernable rage, at the thought of being robbed of a swamp of which they had never heard, that only a first-class European war would bring them the relief for which their natures craved. They decided against this; thus postponing until 1914 Europe's Greatest Joke.

At this point the Elder Statesman interrupts to say that I have got the whole thing wrong. There is no suggestion (he says) that war is the natural expression of individual emotion; but it *is* the natural expression of national emotion. Just as it is natural for an individual to achieve his ends by force, if he cannot achieve them in any other way; so it is natural for a nation in the last resort to use force to achieve its ends.

Let us consider this.

When we say that certain conduct is natural we mean presumably, that it is in accordance with human nature. But for some reason we always identify human nature with the lowest instincts of the animal. It is 'only human nature' to be cruel; never to be kind. Greediness is natural; but not restraint. It is human nature to resent; it is not human nature to forgive. Readers of *Punch* may remember the joke in which the owner of a dog, which has snapped at a little girl who teased it, says apologetically to the indignant mother: 'After all, the dog's only human.' To be 'human', apparently, is to forget that we have souls and intelligences, to forget that we have aspirations towards immortality, and to remember only that we are descended from the monkeys.

Very well. Let it be so for the moment. We are animals. But, even so, does the analogy of the 'naturalness of war' hold?

If a mouse wants cheese, it naturally takes it wherever it is to be found, without bothering about the ownership of the cheese. But when once a mouse has learnt the nature of a mouse-trap, does it still go into a mouse-trap after cheese?

If a cat wants to go quickly from one place to another, it naturally goes as quickly as it can, regardless of whether it is trespassing on somebody else's property. But if there are puddles in the way, it does not go through the puddles. And if there is a dog at the other end, it does not go there at all.

In other words, it is part of the nature of animals to *count the cost* of their actions, in so far as their instincts or their intelligences give them guidance. Makers of war, as I have tried to show, do not count the cost of war. Conceding to the Elder Statesman (as, in fact, I do not concede) that an act can be natural to a corporate body which is unnatural to its individual members ; admitting that the possession of Fashoda would have some national value either to England or to France ; it remains contrary to all that we know, both of human nature and of animal nature, to seek its possession in the wildly disproportionate hazard of a war.

2

But, indeed, there is no reason to take the Elder Statesman so seriously, for again and again he himself has made it clear that war is an entirely unnatural convention. As I am writing this chapter he comes to my rescue yet once more.

Listen to him in a leading article in *The Times* :

' Finally there is universal abhorrence of the idea that civilized nations should sink to methods of barbarism to the extent of making war upon one another by bombardment from the air. It is sometimes lightly argued that bombardment from the air is no worse than artillery bombardment. Materially and morally it is infinitely worse. Its destruction must be more indiscriminate, and once action has been engaged it would involve women and children and the accumulated wealth of civilization in slaughter and ruin. It would be the bankruptcy of statesmanship to admit that it is a legitimate form of warfare for a nation to destroy its rival's capital from the air, and that the correct procedure of the attacked nation is to destroy the attacker's capital and all the life in it with high-explosive, noxious and bacteriological bombs.'

Or in other words :

' War is indiscriminate, but it must not be too indiscriminate. It may destroy towns, but not capitals. It may involve women and children in Scarborough, but not in London, where it would also involve editors. " Materially and morally " bombardment from the air is " infinitely " worse than bombardment from the land ; morally, that is to say, because materially. Let us, therefore, amend the Rules of War.'

Now here are a few facts about the Rules of War :

(*a*) The conduct of war is subject to certain rules agreed upon by all European nations.

(*b*) It is certain that any nation which feels that it can achieve victory by so doing will disregard any rule which it finds inconvenient.

(*c*) It is equally certain that it will accuse the enemy of having broken the rule first.

(*d*) The enemy, if it has not already broken it, will now hasten to do so.

(*e*) Before the last war the use of gas was prohibited. Germany used gas, alleging that gas had been used against her.

(*f*) All the other nations then used gas.

(g) *If a new rule is made prohibiting bombardment of a capital from the air, the prohibition will be ignored by the first nation which finds it convenient, and safe, to ignore it.*

(h) *All the other combatant nations will then ignore it.*

To which may be added :

(i) *Such bombardments will bring agonizing deaths to thousands, perhaps millions, of the defenceless, the majority of whom will be women and children.*

(j) *If, as is probable, this is the end of civilization, it will not greatly matter which disintegrating nation is alleged to have been responsible.*

All this is common knowledge. Now what is the peace-lover's reaction to it?

He says:

' I have always thought that war was wrong. If everybody else had thought so, it would have been abolished. Unfortunately there were many who did not share my views; but even they will hardly stand for the indiscriminate torture of their women and children. If only I can bring home to them that this is what modern war inevitably means, then at last they will share my hatred of it, and between us we shall establish peace.'

What is the Elder Statesman's reaction?

He seems to be thinking:

'The indiscriminate slaughter of women and children is horrible. There was none of this in my young days. It gives quite a false impression of war; and, if it goes on, it is probable that the common people will refuse to stand for it any longer.'

And then what does he say? Does he express delight that the common people may refuse to stand for it any longer? Does he help them to come to this decision by ramming into their minds the well-known, well-proved fact that when once a war is begun a nation will stop at nothing to achieve victory? Does he tell them that, as a consequence of this, any future war must mean horrible deaths for the defenceless?

No.

He says, or seems to be saying:

'The indiscriminate slaughter of Elder Statesmen is also horrible; and the destruction of their offices and their clubs. If war is to mean this, then obviously it must be abolished. But are things necessarily as bad as they seem? Couldn't we agree to abolish bombardment from the air, and keep to the old style of war, which, materially and morally, was so infinitely better? Then, when a statesman gets his country entangled in a war in the old conventional way, we shan't have silly sentimental protests from Pacifists about the wickedness and cruelty of it. Because then only soldiers will be killed, and, as I have pointed out to soldiers so often, *Dulce et decorum est pro patria mori.*'

This is what he seems to be saying; and it destroys the whole case for the naturalness and inevitability of war, giving it at once the artificiality of a game. For if it is 'natural' for Germany to seek what is called victory by bombarding Paris with big guns, how can it be 'unnatural' for France to avoid what is called defeat by retaliating on Berlin in the only method possible—with aeroplanes? Human nature works just the other way. It is entirely unnatural that men should fight, with all the elaborate deliberation of war, for a fever-haunted swamp four thousand miles away which none of them knew that they wanted. But when the war is begun; when they are fighting, not now for a political chimera, but for something which they know and love and understand, the inviolability (as they see it) of their country; when the killing is at its height, and all their passions are aroused, their fierce stubbornness and resentment of defeat; then it is entirely natural, human nature being what it is, and men being men and not saints, that they should grasp at the one certain means of victory, even if, in the calmness of academic debate some years ago, an elderly statesman has promised conditionally that they wouldn't.

2

A further study of this quotation from *The Times* throws light, not only on the conventionality of war, but on the conventional acceptance of war to which politicians, patriots and clergymen have accustomed themselves.

'*There is universal abhorrence of the idea that civilized nations should sink to methods of barbarism to the extent of making war upon one another by bombardment from the air.*'

'Methods of barbarism' is almost breath-taking in its ingenuousness. Bombardment from the air is not noticeably a feature of barbaric warfare, but, as barbaric tribes have discovered to their cost, it is an extremely noticeable feature of civilized warfare. Up to now barbaric tribes have not sunk to our level, but if ever they do, it will be the civilized nations who will be responsible.

'*It is sometimes lightly argued that bombardment from the air is no worse than artillery bombardment. Materially and morally it is infinitely worse.*'

But if morally it is infinitely worse (and if, as is often the case, *The Times* speaks with the effective voice of England), why does England not renounce this infinitely worse crime? How can an infinite immorality be less degrading because it is shared with other nations, or, for this reason, more consistent with the honour of any one nation? By all means let England try to persuade other nations to share her renunciation of the infinitely immoral. That is the part of the good missionary. But missionaries do not allow their morality to depend upon the receptivity of the heathen. ' Let's *all* give up head-hunting, I will if you will ' is not their usual formula.

'*It would involve women and children and the accumulated wealth of civilization in slaughter and ruin.*'

But why not? Isn't that the idea of war? Why do nations fight if not to bring about the complete surrender of the conquered to the will of the conqueror? How is that surrender obtained if not by deliberate slaughter and ruin? And hasn't war always involved women and children? How many millions of women and children were involved in the last war? Leaving out the numberless dead, what of the women who lost all that life held for them, what of the children for whom life will never hold anything?

'*It would be the bankruptcy of statesmanship to admit that it is a legitimate form of warfare for a nation to destroy its rival's capital from the air.*'

As soon as we begin making rules for war, as soon as we say that this is legitimate warfare and that the other is not, we are admitting that war is merely an agreed way of settling an argument. The excuse of 'human nature' is no longer available. A natural fight, a fight between animals, is a fight, tooth and claw, to the death. By the moral standards of war everything is legitimate. If, however, nations can agree not to bomb each other's capitals from the air, let them so agree. But it would be no more difficult to agree not to bomb anything from the air; to agree not to fight in the air; to agree not to fight at all. It has been suggested that a law against bombing from the air could be enforced more easily than a law against any other form of warfare, for the reason that an offender against the law could be immediately bombed by all the other signatory nations. But any nation which engaged in war at all (contrary to agreement) could be immediately bombed by all the other nations. Moreover, the 'other nations' would have much more difficulty in judging an infraction of a bombing agreement (which would take place in war-time) than an infraction of a no-war agreement (which would take place in peace-time). Would they drop bombs on Paris at the word of the Wolff Bureau that Berlin had been bombed? Or would they want photographs, or the evidence of neutrals? How easy for Germany to provide the evidence: an unimportant, carefully evacuated area of the town bombed by a few of their own aeroplanes disguised as French! What a delightfully safe way of getting the enemy's capital bombed at somebody else's expense! ... Finally, what happens if all the signatory nations are themselves engaged in the war from the beginning—as they would have been in 1914?

'*The bankruptcy of statesmanship*'!

As if its fraudulent bankruptcy needed more proof than has been given in the last fifty years!

4

Sympathetic Reader. Forgive me for interrupting, but are you not proving too much?

M. In what way?

S.R. You implied in an earlier chapter that war was entirely contrary to the divine in man.

M. Yes.

S.R. In this chapter you are saying that it is entirely contrary to the animal in man.

M. Yes.

S.R. Then since men must follow either their divine or their animal impulses, you would now seem to have proved that there is no such thing as war at all. As we know that this is not the case, we are led to assume that men deliberately subdue their natural impulses simply in order to kill each other. It seems—unnatural.

M. Wait.

S.R. What I mean is, human nature must come into it somewhere.

The Sympathetic Reader is right. Human nature does come into it.

1. It is entirely in accordance with human nature that men should enjoy the sense of power. In the conduct of a war men in authority experience that sense of power in the highest degree.

2. It is entirely in accordance with human nature (as the late Lord Birkenhead pointed out) that men should be attracted by the ' glittering prizes ' of war. The glittering prizes are reserved for the men in authority.

3. It is entirely in accordance with human nature that men should be heroically indifferent to pains and horrors which they are not themselves going to encounter. Men in authority are carefully sheltered from the pains and horrors of war.

Furthermore :

1. It is entirely in accordance with human nature that ordinary men should save themselves the labour of thought by accepting traditional beliefs.

2. It is entirely in accordance with human nature that ordinary men should be deceived into acceptance of an evil by its slow but relentless growth from something less evil.

3. It is entirely in accordance with human nature that ordinary men should follow the line of least resistance by submitting themselves to men in authority : particularly when this sub-

mission provides an outlet for their natural sentimentality.

War is an unnatural resultant of all these natural forces.

To give another example:

It is natural for the owner of a high-powered car to wish to drive as fast as possible.

It is natural for a brain-worker, absorbed in his work, to walk out of his house still thinking of his work.

It is natural for him to cross the road if he wants to get to the opposite pavement.

But it is not natural for him to commit suicide.

We can prevent such suicides, either by controlling the traffic or by waking up the pedestrian.

War can be prevented as soon as the ordinary man awakes to its realities, or the man in authority controls those animal instincts which he calls human nature.

CHAPTER XII

AGGRESSION AND DEFENCE

I

IT is not easy to awake the ordinary man to realities, for the last thing which he cares to surrender is his habit of thought. In 1909 Bleriot flew the Channel. Twenty-five years later we are being exhorted to become 'air-minded'. In 1900 motor-cars began to come into general use. Thirty years later we are in process of becoming speed-conscious, realizing, but only now, that roads designed for horse-drawn traffic are unfitted for motor traffic. With these developments in inter-communication, with the facilities of modern machinery, the work of the world can now be done in half the time which it used to take. But we shall be many more years before we adapt our philosophy of labour to these modern conditions.

Universal peace may have seemed an impossible dream to our forefathers, but in their days war was not the impossible nightmare which it is now become. Nor was their war Universal War. The problem which confronts Europe to-day is not to be solved by the easy generalities of the past. Only a mind dulled by the rust of centuries can allow itself to think that war is human nature; that the only way of avoiding it is to prepare for it; and that when one has affirmed these two great principles one has no further responsibility for anything which happens.

What will assuredly happen is another war.

Within the last few months a well-known General has made his contribution to this next war. He said:

'There is only one way of ensuring peace, and that is to be so much stronger than the other fellow that he daren't attack you.'

There may be a Wonderland, or a fourth dimension, in which it is possible for every nation to be stronger than every other nation, but it is not to be found in this world. Moreover (as may have occurred to the General after he had sat down), in modern war nations form alliances. To be stronger than the other fellow is not enough; one must be stronger than all the other fellows put together. An armament race in which every European Power is feverishly seeking security by outmatching any combination of all the other Powers is not so much a guarantee of peace as a guarantee that Europe is one vast lunatic asylum.

Unfortunately the General's attitude of mind is not an uncommon one. To the average Englishman the problem of peace is the problem of not being invaded. To prevent invasion he demands a large Navy, a large Air Force and (apparently) a Cadet Corps in every public school. This being so, he cannot blame the average Frenchman, German and Italian for demanding the same things. For England's honour is not held in such high esteem by other nations, England's record in the past is not considered so spotless, that the belief of English clergymen, English generals and English editors in the pacific quality of English armaments is going to bring the rest of Europe complete reassurance. Bombs and battleships have a way of looking offensive to ' the other fellow ', however pacifically they are designed. Whatever its nationality, a defensive bayonet has the same unpleasant appearance as an aggressive one.

If, then, we are to avoid another war, we must give one entirely new thought the right of entry into our minds. It is this :

Preparations for defence are as dangerous to the cause of peace as preparations for aggression.

Until we are accustomed to this thought, there will be no security for civilization.

The Elder Statesman will protest indignantly ; just as, in a previous chapter, our Churchman

AGGRESSION AND DEFENCE

protested. He will say that there is a vast distinction between aggression and defence; that a defensive war is as obviously right as an aggressive war is wrong.

Very well.

What is a defensive war? Presumably a war in defence of something. In defence of what?

One answer, of course, is *Territory*. But even if all wars were territorial wars, it would not follow that the defender of territory was in the right. If Germany had won the last war, and had annexed Belgium, would a subsequent war for the liberation of Belgium have been wrong and aggressive? As it happened, the Allies won the war, and France annexed Alsace-Lorraine. Will a subsequent attempt by Germany to regain Alsace be defensive and right? What is the answer?

It may be said by Englishmen that Belgium has a 'right' to her own integrity, and that France's 'right' to Alsace-Lorraine was not prejudiced by anything which happened in 1870. But are nations always in agreement about each other's rights? What is the truth about Germany's right to German East Africa? And what, we may ask, is the truth about Spain's right to Gibraltar? On this line of argument the difference between aggression and defence is no more than any difference of opinion about anything; and war remains, as it has always been, merely a clumsy and barbarous and expensive way of ending a difference of opinion.

Wars, however, are not always fought in pursuit or defence of territory. A ' tariff war ' may lead to an ultimatum. Then which nation is attacking and which defending ? In a sense each is defending its rights, for each will proclaim the right to live, and allege that the other is endangering it. Wars may be declared, as Austria declared war on Servia, in defence of some supposed prestige. It was generally admitted that Austria had the right to some sort of ' satisfaction ' for the ' insult ' of Serajevo, and it was, in fact, the clash between Austria's ' defence ' of her original claim and Servia's ' defence ' against an excessive claim which led to the Great War.

It is clear then, that, whatever the origin of a war, each country can protest that she is not the aggressor ; each country can claim that she is ' resisting ' an unfair demand, ' defending ' her prestige, or ' repelling ' an attack upon her rights. It is also clear that with the modern facilities for organizing and distributing lies, which every government possesses and none scruples to use, the justice of a cause can be firmly established in the minds of all nationals fighting for it. If the countries of Europe are going to limit themselves in the future to defensive wars ; if they are going to limit themselves to wars for which God's approval has been obtained in advance by their clergy; they will not be pledged to one single war less. To justify defensive war is automatically to justify the next war in which one's own country is engaged, and is, therefore, automatically to justify war.

But there is another reason why any distinction made between aggressive and defensive preparations for war leaves no hope of peace. As I said in a previous chapter, no nation trusts the word of another nation. It is not surprising that statesmen should be cynical about the good faith of each other, when they have been given such abundant reason for cynicism. If there is one sin which brings its own punishment, it is the sin of lying. Truth is the supreme virtue, and it is because we have allowed politicians to neglect it at the call of a false patriotism that we have been burdened with this nightmare of war.

For it is the simple fact that no statesman, no general, has ever hesitated to lie if the good of the state seemed to demand it. When periodically there is an outcry against the sale of honours, every leader of every party blandly professes ignorance of such sale. They are lying; we know that they are lying; but it is not a matter of adverse comment. The convention is that their personal honour is untouched if the lies which they tell are in the interest of the state. When, in war, a general orders an attack which is repulsed with hideous losses, he announces that 'all goes well with British arms'. It is a lie—but *pro patria*. 'I could not love thee, dear, so much, loved I not honour more', said Lovelace to his lady. Unfortunately no Patriot has ever addressed his country so.

This is traditional. Even in home politics, still more in international politics, the ordinary standards of honour have never applied. One could not imagine the craziest Patriot praying that his son should grow up 'as honourable as England'. International politics is a morass of treachery, theft, broken promises, lies, evasions, bluff, trickiness, bullying, deliberate misunderstanding and shabby attempts to get an opponent into a false position. Our whole conception of national morality is different from our conception of private morality. Consider, as one trivial example of this difference, the war-debt between England and America. If this had been a debt contracted between two honourable men in analogous circumstances, the one would have been as insistent on paying it as the other would have been scornful of accepting payment. As it is, we have an excited discussion, every six months or so, as to whether England should, or should not, keep her word. Imagine a similar discussion in a family which considered its honour to be above reproach!

AGGRESSION AND DEFENCE

Now we cannot have it both ways. We cannot disregard truth and expect to be trusted. By its lack of candour in the past every nation has surrendered to its enemies the right of interpretation of its actions. For England to maintain a large navy and a large air-force : to asseverate that she is keeping them ' solely for defensive purposes ' : and to expect any other country to believe her is to exhibit an ingenuousness unworthy even of the nursery. Armaments in the hands of a foreign nation will always be aggressive armaments : partly because no faith is possible between statesmen who put their country above their honour ; partly because, with the best faith in the world, there can never be agreement as to what is aggression and what defence.

2

It is useless, therefore, for nations to agree among themselves (as some of them have done) to use their armaments only for defensive purposes. As soon as an occasion of war arises between two nations, each will accuse the other of being the aggressor, each will accuse the other of being the first to cross the frontier, each will accuse the other of firing the first shot or dropping the first bomb. Then and thereafter the nationals of each country will be convinced that their country is the innocent and defensive one.

To renounce aggression is not enough. We must also renounce defence.

It is a hard and uncomfortable thought, but at least it must be allowed circulation.

Having given it a moment's circulation in his mind, the Elder Statesman will ask me if I also suggest renouncing the police.

No.

'But don't you see', he says, 'that a military force, used defensively as England uses it, is merely a glorified police-force? If you forbid a country to manufacture defensive armaments, then any marauder can take advantage of her defencelessness. Just as a burglar would take advantage of a defenceless community in which there were no police.'

Now this comparison of armies with policemen is constantly made, and as constantly answered. I shall answer it again, because it is important that the falseness of the comparison should be made clear.

A burglar breaks into a house and steals the spoons. A policeman is called in. The burglar is arrested and brought to trial.

Who tries him? Not the policeman.

Who punishes him? Not the policeman.

Perhaps the burglar pleads that the spoons found in his bag were his own spoons, stolen from him by the householder some years ago. Who decides

AGGRESSION AND DEFENCE

on the real ownership of the spoons ? Not the policeman.

All that the policeman does is to force the offender to submit to trial by somebody else.

But an armed nation, however defensively acting, acts in the combined rôles of householder, policeman, judge and burglar. It is invaded ; it arrests the invader ; it sentences him to punishment . . . and then it picks his pockets.

Now the Elder Statesman rejects violently the idea that his country should renounce defensive war. His country, he says, cannot be left open to attack. Even if the comparison of an army with a police-force is not strictly accurate, at least an armed nation can be compared with an armed householder ; and a householder is entitled to resist an attack on his property.

True. But is the Elder Statesman content that his country should limit herself to the rights of an armed householder ? When the armed householder has subdued the intruder, he leaves the judgment of the intruder to a disinterested third party, to whom it is a matter of personal indifference whether certain silver spoons belong to this man or to that. In the event of an attack being made upon, and successfully repelled by, his country, is the Elder Statesman willing that the subsequent Peace Terms should be drawn up by (say) the King of Sweden ?

Will he, in fact, give this pledge to the rest of Europe:

'*If ever England should be engaged in another war, she will not, if victorious, dictate the terms of Peace, but will leave them to some impartial court in some neutral country to determine.*'

When England has given that pledge, then, and only then, will she be able to regard her fighting services as an international police-force.

Meanwhile, the Elder Statesman may ask himself what would have happened if, at the end of the last war, the victorious Allies (all of them, he would say, acting solely on the defensive, and in the interests of Justice) had allowed an impartial Court to draw up the terms of peace. Would it have been the Peace of Versailles?

Let him also ask himself how many of the Allies would have fought in the war at all if they had been fighting as a police-force.

Would Italy have fought?
Would Rumania?
Would France?

It is almost comic, is it not, to think of all these disinterested policemen?

3

If every nation renounces not only aggression but defence: renounces, that is, the use of armaments : how are nations to settle their differences ? Obviously by arbitration.

There seem to be three main objections in the Patriot's mind to the idea of Universal Arbitration.

1. It is not in keeping with the dignity of a great nation to submit a dispute involving its sovereign rights to the arbitrament of another nation.

2. A Neutral Court would never be an impartial Court, since it would either be composed of nationals of a country which was within the orbit of one of the disputants, or it would be composed of individuals of various countries, all of whom would have their own national or personal prejudices.

3. A nation which had lost its case could not be depended upon to accept the verdict peaceably.

And as a rider to his last proposition, the Patriot would add : ' What about Germany ? '

Now it is possible that even the most sympathetic reader has been saying to himself with every page that he reads : ' What about Germany ? '—meaning by that : ' What is the good of talking about peace, and the abolition of armaments, and morality, and common sense : what is the good of reasoning at all so long as Germany remains in her present state of mind ? Abolish Germany, and there might be some hope of abolishing war. But unless you can do that——'

Very well, then. Before we consider the normal objections to arbitration, let us, in the next chapter try to abolish Germany. Let us, that is to say, try to abolish the German bogey which Hitler has left behind him at Geneva.

CHAPTER XIII

FASCIST INTERLUDE

IT is an interesting fact, which is often forgotten, that the object of War is to impose Peace. In 1918 Turkey surrendered to the Allies. In 1922 we were very nearly at war with Turkey again. Two of the reasons given in excuse for another war were the need for ' securing the freedom of the Straits ' and the desirability of ' preserving the sanctity of our graves in Gallipoli '. It must have occurred to many people that, if we could not secure the freedom of the Straits and preserve the sanctity of our graves in Gallipoli after defeating the Turks completely in 1918, there was no reason why we should be any more successful if we defeated them completely again in 1922. The situation seemed to be that we were very good at making war with Turkey, but that we were entirely unable to make any sort of peace with Turkey.

The situation seems to be much the same as regards Germany. For many years up to 1914 Germany was considered to be ' a menace to the peace of Europe '. It was intended that the Great War should put an end to this menace. Most of the volunteers who were Pacifists at heart fought in the war for no other reason than that it was (we were assured) a war to end war. By 1918 we had defeated Germany. As far as one country can ever be at the mercy of other countries, she was in that lowly position . . . and we might almost say that, from that day until this, Europe has been terrified of the defeated Germany.

If nothing which I have written in this book has made war look silly, this fact should make war look silly: that after a struggle which cost thousands of millions of pounds and over ten million lives, the nation which (as we say) started the war, the nation which was completely defeated in the war, is the nation which, once again, is the chief danger to peace. If war means, not peace, but merely another war, what is the object of it? It has been suggested, quite seriously, that France would be justified now in declaring a 'defensive war' against Germany. To what purpose, if, within a few years, she had to declare another defensive war? And if, in this series of defensive wars, she were to make one unsuccessful war, then presumably it would be Germany's turn, as the victor, to start a series of defensive wars.

FASCIST INTERLUDE

It is probable, then, war being the ineffective instrument it is, that Germany, as a defeated and revengeful nation, would have been considered, in any case, a menace to peace. But, with the rise to power of Hitler, she becomes ten times more threatening. For she makes no secret now of her will to war. A Professor of Geography explains, yet once again, how England is to be invaded; from time to time Goebbels speaks eloquently (though not from personal knowledge) of the ecstasy of bearing sons for the battlefield; and at the regular intervals Goering, that 'clamorous harbinger of blood and death', succumbs, without any regard to privacy, to the verbal menstruation which his nature seems to demand. How (it is asked) can we hold argument with men like these? What hope is there in talking peace to the servants of Hitlerism?

2

Hitlerism is Fascism adapted to the special needs of Germany. For its medieval attitude to war we have higher authority than the evacuations of a Goering or the frothings of a Professor of Geography. We have the words of Mussolini himself. From the *Fascist Encyclopædia* Mr. Wickham Steed has translated him as follows:

' Fascism does not believe either in the possibility or in the utility of perpetual peace. It therefore disavows the principle of pacifism, which counsels a renunciation of struggle and a feeling of cowardice in regard to sacrifice. War alone brings all human energies to their highest tension, and stamps the mark of nobility on those peoples who have the courage to face it. All other ordeals are but substitutes which never place a man face to face with himself in the alternative of death. Hence a doctrine that is based upon the premise of peace is foreign to Fascism.'

This typical Salute to Sentimentality merits no serious examination. After the last war the mark of nobility is stamped so indelibly on the nations of Europe that they can afford now not to bother about it. It is probable, moreover, that those of their nationals to whom life is not one long Roman salute do not set much store by an order of nobility in which the more backward States of South America take, unchallenged, the highest rank. And, of course, there *are* ordeals, other than the ordeal of making speeches to the troops in war-time, which place a man face to face with himself in the alternative of death. Thinking differently from a Fascist leader in peace-time is one of them. Finally, pacifism does not counsel a renunciation of struggle and a feeling of cowardice in regard to sacrifice. It struggles against a renunciation of the use of the intelligence; it counsels some slight feeling of decency in regard to the sacrifice of women and children; it counsels recognition of the fact that we have a lifetime of struggle in front of us to get the world right after the last war, and that another war would achieve what the last war so nearly achieved: the end of civilization.

But though in one sense we cannot take such rhetoric seriously, in another sense we cannot take it seriously enough. For the serious thing is, not that Fascist leaders should show as little awareness of reality as the hero of a boy's adventure story, but that they should have in their own hands the power of giving practical expression to their romanticism. If this is the faith of Mussolini and of Hitler, and if they wish to put their faith, as they can, into action, what hope is there for the peace of Europe?

To discover this it is necessary to consider, however briefly, the bases of Fascism.

3

In the democratic creed the State exists for the benefit of the individual. In the Fascist creed the individual exists for the benefit of the State. Mussolini claims that he has substituted the Twentieth Century 'Rights of the State' for the Nineteenth Century 'Rights of Man'. What he has really done is to substitute the Rights of One Man for the Rights of Every Man. The private

Italian has surrendered freedom of thought, freedom of speech, freedom of action. Mussolini has surrendered none of these things. On the contrary he has acquired a greatly enlarged freedom: the freedom to think, speak and act, not only for himself, but for everybody else. *L'état, c'est moi.* The Rights of the State are the Rights of Mussolini.

This confusion of the Rights of the State with the Rights of the Autocrat was a natural rather than an inevitable consequence of Fascism. The twentieth-century doctrine of the Rights of the State need not have included autocracy; the post-War discovery that only an autocrat can 'get things done' need not have meant the surrender of the individual to the State. But since the first 'thing' which the autocrat wants to 'get done' is the surrender of the individual to himself, it was natural for Mussolini to identify his own needs with the needs of the State, and to proclaim in its present form the new twentieth-century doctrine. For only thus, in this democratic twentieth century, can an autocracy be established.

Fascism, then, is simply autocracy up to date. Being an autocracy it is based on force. It follows that the force must always be there: a standing army of adherents in suitably coloured shirts, devoted either to the autocrat himself or to the State through the autocrat. To keep the devotion of this army at its height all the picturesqueness of real war must be invoked : the salute and the uniform, the speeches, the banners and the war-songs : even, from time to time, the intoxication of victory over an elderly Jew or an outnumbered political opponent. That such an army should have occasional longings to ' bring its human energies to a higher tension ' is natural. Of necessity it was nourished on the sentimentalities of war ; inevitably its thoughts will turn to war.

It is equally necessary that the people as a whole —those outside the standing army—should be educated to think of war as their divine mission. For they must think of something as their divine mission, and what other divine mission can they have ? It is true that tourists, writing in *The Times*, have often claimed in defence of Fascist Italy that the trains arrive more punctually now than they did in the old democratic days ; but there must be inhabitants of the country, less dependent on the movements of the 12.30, who do not feel its punctual arrival to be a sufficient explanation of the surrender of their liberties. They have given themselves to the State for some more holy cause than this. They have given themselves to the State, and what will the State do with them ?

For though man is not, in the sense alleged by the Militarist, a fighting animal, he is certainly a competitive animal. He likes matching himself against his fellows, particularly if he has prepared himself deliberately for that purpose. After three months of intensive training a university crew may be supposed to have accustomed itself to the possibility of a boat race. Indeed, it would be difficult to keep its members in training for this time, if something in the nature of a boat race had not been promised them. Similarly, if the people of a country surrender their liberty to an autocratic trainer on his assurance that their country needs the sacrifice, they require the further assurance that, when the training is completed, their country will take the field against somebody or something. And what decisive field can a country take but the field of battle?

All this sounds most dangerous to the peace of Europe, but in effect the danger cancels itself. A warlike education of the people is seen to be a necessity to the existence of the Fascist State, and for that very reason it is not necessarily a danger to any other state. Members of a team take orders from their captain on the field, but not off; and a stable autocracy is only possible if the autocrat is perpetually leading his men on to the field. 'Surrender your wills to me', cries the Fascist, 'and I will lead the country to victory!' The actual battle is another matter.

Indeed, quite another matter. For, however completely Fascist leaders may seem to have forgotten the horrors of the last war, we may be sure that the supreme horror of war is vividly in their minds : the knowledge that those who lead their country to Armageddon have no chance of surviving defeat and but little hope of enjoying victory. Nothing is more certain in the uncertain future of Europe than that, if Fascist Germany or Fascist Italy is involved in the next war, it will not be a Fascist Germany or a Fascist Italy which will come out of it. Even if (which is unlikely) civilization survives that war ; even if Germany is still a nation and Italy is still a nation ; it is absolutely certain that there will be no Hitler, no Mussolini, to direct their destinies.

And the possibility (if you hold it to be a possibility) that a Fascist leader is entirely selfless, hating this burden of autocracy, but sacrificing himself for his beloved country, makes the horror no lighter for him. For if he is gone, who else is there ? If his beloved country is not Fascist, what hope is there for it ? The more selfless he is, the more determined he must be to preserve his authority. But how can he preserve it without the help of his standing army ? How can Hitler fight Communism and France simultaneously ? He can establish his autocracy by keeping his people at the pitch of self-sacrifice by the promise of war. But he can only preserve it so long as his country is at peace.

Finally let us take comfort from this :

Ten years ago it was generally felt that Italy was the chief menace to the peace of Europe. Few people think so now. Indeed, it would be fair to say that Mussolini is commonly regarded as one of the safeguards of peace. Yet he still feels it necessary, for domestic reasons, to extol the glories of war in such brave words as I have quoted above.

So, if a German Nazi also talks like a boy's adventure story, we need not despair. It is often said that Germany prepares for war while paying lip-service to peace. The truth may be that she prepares for peace while paying lip-service to war.

4

In subsequent chapters, then, I shall assume that Germany is as amenable to reason as Italy (or any other nation), and that, within certain limitations imposed on her by the Versailles Treaty, she is as anxious as any other nation for the security of peace. Let us, on this assumption, consider the objections which the Patriots of every country have raised to the substitution of Settlement by Arbitration for the conventional Settlement by Force.

CHAPTER XIV

ARBITRATION

I

IN Chapter XII I gave the three usual objections to arbitration. Put as concisely as possible, they amount to this :

'Nations wouldn't consent to submit certain matters to a Neutral Court ; they couldn't be sure of an impartial hearing if they did ; and if the verdict went against them, they would resort to war again.'

Which seems to settle the question of arbitration.

Now it must be remembered that compulsory arbitration is not suggested as a charming thing in itself ; it is suggested as an alternative to something extremely unpleasant : war. The alternative to toothache is dentistry. The possibility and desirability of dentistry is not settled by the objection that nobody wants his jaw messed about by a stranger, and how can you be sure that he won't hurt you. Militarist objections to any plan for the prevention of war seem always to be made

ARBITRATION

along these lines. It seems to be assumed that Universal Peace is only worth considering if it is quite easy to come by, and demands no sacrifices from anybody.

Universal Peace will demand many sacrifices. It will demand the sacrifice of a good deal of traditional nonsense. But it will not demand the sacrifice of ten million lives.

2

The first objection to arbitration is this :

A. It is not in keeping with the dignity of a great nation to submit a dispute involving its sovereign rights to the arbitrament of another nation.

England and France disputed over the possession of Fashoda. The objection is made that if England had referred the dispute to Norway (say) for settlement, she would have given a foreign country (Norway) the right of interference in matters which affected her sovereignty. But equally, if she had gone to war with France, she would have given a foreign country (France) the right of interference in matters which affected her sovereignty. In order to keep control of her own destiny, she has, in the one case, to convince Norway of her Right, and, in the other case, to convince France of her Might. Doubtless she would prefer it if she could control her own destiny to the extent of doing anything she liked, and taking anything she wanted, without argument or objection from anybody. Doubtless we should all like this. But when a rival claimant appears, the rival claims have to be submitted to some sort of ordeal, and it is habit and environment, rather than any absolute standards, which make one sort of ordeal preferable to another. If two politicians disagreed as to which of them should be the leader of their party, they would regard it as beneath their dignity to decide the question by a wrestling match on the floor of the House of Commons. But if two all-in wrestlers disagreed as to which of them should be President of the newly formed Professional Wrestlers Club, a wrestling match would seem to them to be the right and dignified way of settling the dispute. What they would consider to be beneath their dignity would be any sort of competitive examination in political economy.

If, then, a country wants something to which some other country makes a claim, there is nothing inherently dignified in referring the claim to the ordeal of war rather than to the ordeal of arbitration; for there can be no inherent dignity in taking a thing by force simply because one is strong enough to do so. Nor is the dignity more apparent in a failure to take a thing by force, because one is not strong enough to do so. On the other hand there does seem to be a certain dignity in relying on the justice of one's claim rather than on one's power to evade all reference to justice.

In these days, when every nation depends not only for its wealth, but even for its existence, on the community of nations, sovereign rights are little more than a phrase, and the patriot's pride of independence is more often comic than admirable. The proud Bolivian considers it to be beneath the dignity of his country to allow her dispute with Paraguay to be settled in European council-halls. . . . It is being settled instead in European armament factories.

3

B. A Neutral Court would never be an impartial Court, since it would either be composed of nationals of a country which was within the orbit of one of the disputants, or it would be composed of individuals of various countries, all of whom would have their own national or personal prejudices.

It is sometimes forgotten that the world has been organized for thousands of years, and still is organized, on a war-basis, not on a peace-basis. There may be many good reasons why a grocer should not sell fish, but the absence of ice in his shop is not one of them. If he decides on fish, he makes it his business to get ice. If Europe decides on arbitration, she makes it her business to get impartial Neutral Courts. The impartiality of a court is largely a matter of tradition. It would not be impossible to build up such a tradition in a roster of courts from every country in Europe. It would not be impossible for each country to keep her Neutral Court supplied with a service of honourable and distinguished men, capable of thinking and speaking in the one agreed language of the courts ; such men to be employed, first as counsel and then as judges. Just as there is a tradition of the sea, acting on which a lifeboatman is proud to risk his life impartially for people of all nationalities ; so there could be a tradition of the Neutral Courts acting on which a judge would be proud to distribute justice impartially to all nations. Loyalty to his profession is one of the strongest loyalties in man. Even if loyalty to his country were stronger, it would be a reinforcing, not an antagonistic, loyalty. Pride of country is not synonymous with pride of arms. It would be a matter of national pride to make one's own court the highest in reputation of all the national courts, so that any two disputing nations would agree that from the Neutral Court of such-and-such a country justice and sympathy and understanding were most certainly to be obtained.

It may be said that one does not come by such a

ARBITRATION

tradition in a day. No doubt in the early stages of the courts injustice might sometimes be done. But it must be remembered that this injustice is to be compared, not with an absolute Justice, but with the 'justice' which obtains as the result of war. Possibly if the Serajevo murders had been referred to a Neutral Court with but little tradition of impartiality behind it, Austria would have complained that she had not had justice done to her. But it is also possible that Austria is not completely satisfied with the justice of her present state; and would have preferred the judgment of that Neutral Court. Sir Galahad is reported by Lord Tennyson as having said that his strength was as the strength of ten because his heart was pure. No nation has shown any signs of achieving that Ten Power Standard. Once the battle is begun, the purity of the cause matters no longer. All that matters is that in every war one side is the loser, and that in every peace the losing side has injustice done to it.

4

C. A nation which had lost its case could not be depended upon to accept the verdict peaceably.

This objection raises at once the question of 'Sanctions'. Let us, then, consider Sanctions.

In an earlier chapter I said that it was as absurd for a country to talk about its honour as it would be for the Multiplication Table to talk about its honour: the reason being that countries can only be represented by statesmen, and that statesmen have a tradition of patriotism which is inconsistent with any sort of morality. Knowing this about each other, statesmen are naturally reluctant to accept each other's word, with the result that when a country (through her statesmen) pledges her honour to do this or that, the natural thought in everybody's mind is: ' But how can we be sure she will keep her pledge if it is inconvenient for her to do so?' Moreover, since statesmen, for centuries, have regarded force as the only valid argument, it is natural that they should immediately transfer their thought into another question: ' By what threat of force can we *compel* her to keep her word?'

The force necessary to make a country keep her word of honour is called Sanctions.

Now if Europe consisted of ten honourable countries, all of which were determined to make an end of war, and one small faithless country which had no intention of keeping the peace, the threat of Sanctions would be a valuable weapon. But as Europe consists of half a dozen powerful and dishonourable countries, none of which seems prepared to make the slightest sacrifice for peace, and a number of smaller dishonourable countries, some war-like, some not, a threat of Sanctions

ARBITRATION

seems to be no more than a quick way of ensuring that a small local war shall become a world war.

Consider the last war.

Austria (to *Servia*): Stop it, or I'll make you.

Russia (to *Austria*): Stop it, or I'll make you.

Germany (to *Russia*): Stop it, or I'll make you.

France (to *Germany*): Stop it, or I'll make you.

Germany (to *France*): Stop saying stop it, or I'll make you.

England (to *Germany*): Stop it, or I'll make you.

This reads like something from a comic opera, but it is exactly what happened; and it gives us a rough idea of Sanctions at work. Sanctions doesn't mean a joint expedition by gun-boat to deal with a Boxer rebellion in China. It means fighting a first-class Power, which may be (probably will be) allied to other first-class Powers. In the Great War, Germany proved that, given the advantage of attack, she was nearly strong enough to engage Europe single-handed. If Europe is going to employ Sanctions to compel Germany, or any other country, to keep her word, she has first to ensure that she is a united Europe, and then to declare a European war.

But how can she ensure that she is a united Europe? What is the good of countries pledging themselves to put Sanctions into operation, if the Sanctions only come into operation when it is proved that countries don't keep their pledges? Why should the one pledge be more likely to be kept than the other?

'Very well,' says the Elder Statesman. 'Have it which way you like. You say that Sanctions are impossible. Whether this be so or not, it must be admitted that Europe has not managed to come to any agreement as to their form and use. Then my third objection to Universal Arbitration still stands. *A nation which had lost its case could not be depended upon to accept the verdict peaceably.*'

The objection does not stand. It just goes round in a circle.

Consider:

E.S. We want peace if we can get it. But how?

M. By accepting Arbitration in every dispute which arises.

E.S. That's all very well, but what's to prevent a country refusing to accept an adverse judgment, and resorting to War?

M. But you said you wanted Peace.

E.S. If we can get it.

M. You can get it by accepting Arbitration in every dispute which arises.

ARBITRATION

E.S. Yes, but what's to prevent a country refusing to accept an adverse judgment, and resorting to War?
M. You said you wanted Peace.
E.S. If we can get it.
M. You can get it by accepting——
And so on interminably.

It will be seen that, if there is any meaning in the Elder Statesman's third objection, all it can mean is this:

'Arbitration is no good, because if nations failed to get what they wanted by arbitration, they would try to take it by force.'

Now Arbitration is suggested as an *alternative* to Force. In this chapter we are considering whether it is, or is not, an acceptable alternative. The objection is made that it would detract from the dignity of nations, and I have tried to answer that objection. The objection is made that it would lead to injustice, and I have answered that objection also. But it is no criticism of Arbitration, as an *alternative* to Force, to say that you can't enforce it.

Let me call apologue in aid again to illustrate my meaning. The customary way of deciding which player in a golf-match shall drive first at the first tee is by tossing. Two novices, who had never heard of this custom, might decide it by the more humanly natural method of fighting. This method would have its disadvantages; for though one of them might be victorious, yet the loser (certainly) and both (probably) would be disabled by injuries from proceeding any further with the game. After some days' interval for recovery, they would try again, and again they would get no farther than the first tee. It might occur to them, after some years of this, that it ought not to be beyond human ingenuity to think of some solution of their difficulty: some method whereby, having met on the first tee to play golf, they could actually play golf. They consult a friend, who expounds to them the great principle of tossing.

The two novices consider this suggestion with care, turning it this way and that in their minds. And then one of them says profoundly:

'Tossing is no good. Because the player who had lost the toss couldn't be depended upon to accept the verdict peaceably.'

To which the only possible answer would be: 'Well, which *do* you want? A fight or a golf-match?'

The only possible answer to the Elder Statesman is: Which does Europe want? Peace or War?

If she wants Peace, she can have it by accepting Arbitration.

ARBITRATION

If she wants War, she can have it by not accepting Arbitration.

Arbitration is a substitute for War. *It is not a substitute for Victory.*

Which do politicians want? War or a substitute for War? At present they seem to divide their time between explaining in one set of words how anxious they are for settlement by agreement, and making it quite clear in another set of words how determined they are not to discard settlement by force. The only Disarmament which they discuss is one which leaves them all securely armed against each other; they discuss no Arbitration but that which is protected in advance by the Sanctions of War.

5

In the garden of the new building for the League of Nations at Geneva there is (or should be) a large avenue: lined, not with trees, but with statues of the great captains of the past: and at one end stands, with drawn sword, a vast symbolic figure of Security, and at the other, with sword half out of the scabbard, a figure, equally vast, but slightly more indeterminate, engraved Sanctions. Up and down, from the one figure to the other, little frock-coated men amble in groups, chattering in a diversity of languages. Each time that they reach the end of the avenue, and are pulled up by one or other of these towering figures, they blink in perplexity at it, rub their eyes, say, 'Ah, yes, of course, we're going the wrong way', and amble back again . . .

They call this : '*Exploring every avenue in the search for Peace.*'

CHAPTER XV

NOTES FOR A PEACE CONFERENCE

I

I HAVE a day-dream in which MM. Ramsay MacDonald, Doumergue, Mussolini and Hitler come to dinner with me. Fortunately they can all talk English. I imagine them as quite ordinary people beneath their importance : people, I mean, to whom one can use ordinary language, expecting to be understood. They might be Smith, Brown, Jones and Robinson : friends of mine to whom I speak as an equal, in words which have a common meaning for us. After dinner, a dinner which has left me a trifle exalted, and my guests a little replete, they form themselves into a Peace Conference. I am allowed to be there as a sort of unofficial Chairman. I am allowed to make the opening speech.

This (I say) is a Peace Conference, and in a little while you four men are going to explore one more avenue together. Before you begin your explorations there is something of which I should like to remind you.

The Peace of Europe is in your hands. I mean just that. I do not mean that it is in the hands of England, France, Germany and Italy. I mean that it is within the power of you four men to give us Peace or War. When you talk, as doubtless you will, of 'the intractability of France', it is the intractability of M. Doumergue of which you speak. The 'menace of Germany' is no more than the menace of Hitler. If you feel that you cannot trust 'perfidious Albion', you are afraid that Ramsay MacDonald will go back upon his word. If 'Italy's need for expansion' is the danger, then the only real danger is Mussolini's need. You are up against no urgent national forces, you are merely up against each other.

Until you get this fact firmly in your minds, every avenue which you explore will be a *cul-de-sac*; for at the end of every approach to Peace stands a monster of your own creation which bars the way.

There is no German bogey but Hitler; no chauvinistic Italy but Mussolini; no intractable France but Doumergue; no perfidious Albion but MacDonald. You four men are not at the mercy of irresistible natural forces, before which you must needs patch up some hasty defence; you are confronted by nothing more terrifying

NOTES FOR A PEACE CONFERENCE

than is to be found amongst yourselves. Sometimes (and it sounds a strange thing to say) you seem to be unaware of your own importance; unaware that the happiness or misery of the world waits upon your word.

You four men. It is useless to pretend that you are carried along by this or that 'wave of national feeling'. Such waves are either of your imagination or your own creation. All that the average man wants is to be left in peace: to live his own life, and to manage his own affairs. No Italian wakes up in the morning and says: 'My God, we must expand'; no Italian but Mussolini. No German wakes up in the morning and says: 'Heavens, we must be pan-Germanic'; no German but Hitler, and those whom Hitler has ordered. If Mussolini wished for Peace, and thought that the way to Peace was by the restoration of Tripoli to Turkey, he could, with no difficulty, convince his people (those of them who knew where Tripoli was, and that it belonged to Italy) of the nobility of their country in making this gesture. You four men are at the mercy of no human nature, no passions, no high enthusiasms but your own. You can bully, charm, harangue your countrymen into a happiness or misery of your own choosing.

Now I suggest that you begin this conference by considering whether you want Peace. I think that this is a point which you have not yet discussed. England has discussed Peace with Honour, France has discussed Peace with Security, Italy has discussed Peace with Bellicosity, and Germany has discussed Peace with Equality, Rectification and a little Revenge. Amidst so many rivals for your attention the meek figure of Peace has hardly been discernible.

In considering whether you want Peace, you will naturally contemplate the alternative—War. But it is useless for you to contemplate abstract war; you must bring your imaginations to bear upon the particular war with which you will be concerned. The next war.

I suppose that you all remember the last war. You remember how Europe lived, and died, during that war. You have seen how Europe has been struggling, ever since, to live. Do you think that Europe can possibly survive another war like the last war? Is it not *absolutely* certain that another European war would mean the complete collapse of civilization?

Well, what do you say?

You may come to the conclusion that the world could easily survive another war. I suggest that, if you so conclude, you should give the world some reassuring pen-picture of your countries as you see them at the end of the war. Mr. MacDonald, for instance, might tell his fellow countrymen

NOTES FOR A PEACE CONFERENCE

something about their income-tax; a matter always of absorbing interest to them. As a result of the last war, it rose from 1*s*. 2*d*. to 6*s*. It is now 4*s*. Presumably after the next war, it will be about 8*s*. 10*d*. Mr. MacDonald can tell us in advance why we need not bother too much about that. But I am hopeful that, when you have all considered the matter carefully, you may be able to put your signatures to the following statement:

'*Without prejudice to our opinions of war in the abstract; without prejudice to the settlement of any matters still in dispute between us; we put it upon record that in a world so sensitively organized: in the economic conditions now existing: with the weapons of destruction now available: another European war would mean the end of civilization. Realizing, therefore, our responsibility, not only to our respective countries but to mankind, we assume as our first duty the complete renunciation of war.*'

It is necessary that the renunciation of war must be kept continually in your minds as the *first* duty of this conference. You must agree upon this point before you consider whether war *can* be abolished, and how, if it can be, it is to be. It is useless to say to yourselves: 'We will agree to renounce war, as soon as some nation comes along with a workable scheme of disarmament.'

The renunciation must be made first, and the method of putting it into action must be discussed afterwards. This is not an unreasonable request to make of you. If a man of moderate income is told (and believes) that the life of his much-loved child can only be saved by an expensive operation, he does not consider first by what economies he can manage to pay for it. He decides on the operation at once, knowing that somehow the money must be found, whatever hardships the provision of it may force upon him. So, when the life of mankind is at stake, it is not unreasonable to call upon you to save that life first, and to consider afterwards how best to reconcile with that safety your ambitions and your patriotisms.

I ask you then to discuss first, not the *possibility* of Universal Peace, but the *necessity* of Universal Peace; by which I mean the necessity arising from present conditions, past experience and the terrible menace of the future. Of all that has been said in your previous conferences: of all that has been written lately about Honour and Security: of all the endless argument that has been heard about Peace and War in these last few years: 90 per cent. might have served Pacifist and Militarist for argument at the first Hague Conference, thirty years ago. The war whose abolition you are now considering is not the war of 1905, which seemed then to mean no more than

NOTES FOR A PEACE CONFERENCE

a little pain and death for soldiers, a little excitement for civilians, and for statesmen and generals a little glory. The war which you are considering now means death to everything humane and civilized and cultured which the slow centuries have built up, death to the liberty and dignity of mankind, death to all the little happinesses of simple folk, death to all the great hopes which men have treasured of a world increasing in knowledge and beauty . . . and here you sit, in whose hands lies deliverance from that death, and all that you are asked to affirm is your willingness to deliver us . . .

Then the Peace Conference settles down to discuss bows and arrows again.

2

E.S. What do you mean by 'bows and arrows'?

M. I will explain.

And just as I am wondering how to begin, Lord Rothermere comes to my help. In the *Observer's* 'Sayings of the Week' I read the following:

'At the present moment, which may prove to be the eve of another Armageddon, we are not ready.—*Viscount Rothermere.*'

Now here are two statements, whose truth, for the moment, we will accept.

PEACE WITH HONOUR

1. *The present moment may prove to be the eve of another Armageddon.*
2. *We are not ready.*

Which of these two facts is of the more importance to civilization?

The one overmastering horror of civilization, of Christianity, of mankind is the thought of another Armageddon; the one overmastering concern of statesmen at Peace Conferences is that their particular nation shall be ready for it. They might still be in togas, saying to each other solemnly: 'At the present moment, which may prove to be the eve of another Carthaginian invasion, we are short of hoplites.'

If we are on the eve of another Armageddon, then we are on the eve of the destruction of the world. That is absolutely certain. And, on the eve of the destruction of the world, the Great Statesmen of the world (God help the world) still yammer sentimental, schoolboy rubbish about dignity and honour and prestige; and the Greatest Statesman of Them All, instead of editing *The Boys Own Paper*, proposes to defend 'the greatness of the Italian people' with 'the song of our machine-guns'. Above them towers the mighty, disintegrating cliff, and in its shadow they argue about their little wrestling-matches, and which shall take his braces off first; each of them with only one fixed idea in his head: that he shall not be the losing one when a thousand tons of rock have crashed on to them from above.

That is what I mean by bow-and-arrow talk: the world as it was two thousand years ago, and half a dozen tribes having a pow-wow to see if they can't postpone hostilities until they have got the harvest in. It is in this spirit that Europe discusses Peace in 1934.

3

Sympathetic Reader : In theory you are perfectly right, but in practice—— Well, can't you be a little more practical? This is 1934. Here are the Four Great Men. Here, if you like, are representatives of all the other nations. Well, who does what first? Give us your notes for a real Peace Conference.

M. I was about to do so.

Notes for a Peace Conference in 1934.

1. The Conference should consider first the probable course and results of 'another Armageddon', consulting for this purpose the highest military and economic authorities available. Marshal Foch has said: 'The next war will be a world war. Almost every country will take part in it, and the combatants will include, not only the manhood but the women and children of each nation.' Mr. Baldwin is one of the many who

have said that civilization cannot possibly survive such a war. The Conference should consider these and all other authoritative opinions, and issue a statement of its conclusions. If these conclusions are not unanimous, the beliefs of each nation should be put separately on record. It is understood that the effect of war on Europe as a whole is to be considered; not its effect on a particular nation in the particular circumstance of 'victory' or 'defeat'.

2. If the Conference comes to the conclusion that the next war will be fatal to Europe and the world, then, presumably, it will come to the conclusion that there must be no next war.

3. Each nation should then be asked the following question: 'Would you be prepared to renounce war entirely (*i.e.* both aggressive and defensive war) as far as Europe is concerned, provided that every other European nation were to make the same renunciation with a good faith equal to your own?'

4. It would probably be found that some nations would be willing, in theory, to give this conditional pledge, and that some nations would be unwilling. That is to say: some nations are *contented* with their present position, and are only anxious to be left in peace; and other nations are *discontented* with their present position, and cannot renounce the idea of improving it by the only means known

NOTES FOR A PEACE CONFERENCE

to them—namely, the traditional means of war. The discontented nations should then be asked to state the conditions under which they would give the pledge.

[For example : a German condition might be the restoration of her colonies.]

5. The contented nations concerned should consider to what extent they could satisfy the discontented nations. They should consider this in the light of their determination that there is to be no ' next war ', and on the assumption that the concessions which they make are an absolute assurance of Peace.

[As an example of a ' concession ', and the method of considering it, take the improbable case of a Spanish claim to Gibraltar. Normally, every patriotic Englishman would be horrified at the idea of surrendering Gibraltar ; but these are not normal circumstances. It must be remembered (*a*) that, in as far as Gibraltar's value to England is a military value, nothing of value is being surrendered if Peace is assured ; and (*b*) if Gibraltar has any other value, it can only be measured against the £7,000,000,000 and 1,000,000 lives which the last war cost England. If, in the last resort, England had to choose between Universal Peace and Gibraltar, and chose Gibraltar, then at least we should know how much England wanted Peace.]

6. If deadlock is reached, the exact circumstances should be made public to the world : *i.e.* which nations were 'discontented'; for what concessions they asked; what concessions were granted by each nation, and what refused.

7. In the event of the failure of the Conference, the responsible leader of each country should make a statement to the world, not as a national leader, but as one of those on whose policy the future of the world depends.

[If, for instance, Mussolini genuinely feels that it doesn't matter what happens to the rest of the world as long as Italy is all right, then he should say so, and explain why he thinks Italy will be all right if the rest of the world crashes; or, alternatively again, why he thinks that Italy can engage in a European war without dragging the rest of Europe into it. If, as is possible, he were to think that some concession by Italy, which would bring Peace and happiness to the rest of Europe, was, in some odd way, dishonourable to his country, then he should explain whether this was his private conception of honour, which he intended to force upon his country, or whether the majority of his people shared it.]

8. Throughout the Conference the following facts should be kept continuously in mind.

(*a*) Never in the history of the world has Europe been so unfitted to bear the disruption of a war, and the after-effects of war, as she is now.

(*b*) From now onwards, even more surely than in 1914, any war between two European nations will immediately involve other nations, and in its after-effects will disorganize, probably to breaking point, the whole civilized world.

(*c*) *Every delegate is responsible, therefore, not only to his own country, for his actions, but to civilization.*

Elder Statesman. Very interesting. I see that you have made no provision for the discussion of the one vital difficulty which has confronted every previous Peace Conference.

M. You mean the ' good faith ' of signatory nations to any pledge ?

E.S. Exactly. Again I ask you : How can you be sure that that good faith exists ; and (equally important), even if it does exist, how can you ensure any belief in it ?

M. My contention is that, as long as you assume *bad* faith (which is what every Conference has done so far) you will never arrive anywhere. I suggest, therefore, that this Conference begins by assuming *good* faith, in order to discover if, and how, on this assumption, Universal Peace is possible.

E.S. Very well. Let us agree that, on the

assumption of universal good faith, and faith in each other's good faith, Universal Peace is possible. Then what?

M. Then, in the next chapter, we discuss Patriotism.

E.S. What has that got to do with it?

M. We shall see.

CHAPTER XVI
PATRIOTISM AND PLEDGES

I

THE Patriotism which Patriots claim so loudly for themselves, and deny so freely to others, must not be confused with pride of country. In as far as an English Patriot is proud of England, he is proud of her, not for what she is, but for what he would like her to be. England gave Parliamentary government to the world, but the Patriot is not noticeably proud of Parliamentary government. He is inclined to prefer the Italian model. England makes her characteristic compromise with morality; but the Patriot holds that they order these things better in France. England has her own careless love of games, which the Patriot finds inferior to American concentration; her own methods of business, so much less admirable than German methods. Indeed, when we consider England as she is, we realize that the only thing about her which makes the patriotic bosom swell with pride is the thought that, if she adopted conscription, and if she spent the money, which now she wastes on Education, on an increased Navy and an increased Air Force, then at last she would be a country of which a Patriot could be proud.

Patriotism, then, may be defined as a passionate interest in the military strength of one's country. In a community living on a group of small islands in the Pacific there might be those who loved their island : who were proud of the laws which they had given it, and of the free and happy life which they had made possible. But they would be innocent of Patriotism until somebody suggested that they should all build war-canoes in order to defend themselves against each other. Then the Patriots would stand out as Patriots, and those who were happy in their own island would be exposed as deplorably unpatriotic.

This sort of Patriotism has imposed itself on Europe with the tenacity of an orthodox religion. When the Oxford Union announced that it ' declined in any circumstances to fight for King and Country ', it created even more horror and indignation among Patriots than a motion declining in any circumstances to go to Church would have created among Churchmen. Indeed, a resolution declining in any circumstances to work for England, or declining to live in England, or to love England or be proud of her, would have seemed less horrifying to the Patriot than a refusal to fight for her. For it is only in terms of fighting

PATRIOTISM AND PLEDGES

(and, preferably, in terms of other people fighting) that the Patriot's devotion to his faith can be estimated.

This is the faith which has impressed itself on the world; the faith which now takes precedence of Christianity. When Dr. Johnson said (some years before Mr. Horatio Bottomley was born) that Patriotism was 'the last refuge of a scoundrel', his definition held this much truth: that Patriotism confers on the faithful the same ecclesiastical dispensation which the scoundrel assumes for himself. 'My country, right or wrong' says the Patriot, and, in saying it, gives himself absolution for any wrong done in the name of Patriotism.

It is clear, then, that, as between scoundrels, so between Patriots of different countries, good faith is impossible. Yet it is only on the assumption of universal good faith that Universal Peace is possible. Moreover, it is only on the assumption of war that Patriotism can flourish. Our problem, therefore, may be set out in this way:

War *means* Patriotism.
Patriotism *means* Bad Faith.
Bad Faith *means* War.

Alternatively:

Peace *means* Absence of Patriotism.
Absence of Patriotism *means* Good Faith.
Good Faith *means* Peace.

The problem of the Pacifist has been to discover where, and how, to cut into this vicious circle of War—Patriotism—Bad Faith—War. Which shall he attack first?

In the last chapter I assumed that we had broken into the circle, and had established Good Faith. I suggested that the members of the Peace Conference should make the same assumption, and see where they arrived. The probability is that they would arrive at Peace; for, on the assumption of Good Faith, the two main obstacles in the way, Security and Sanctions, would disappear. If one nation pledges itself not to fight another nation, *and if its word can be trusted*, then the other nation has obtained that much Security; and, since Sanctions are only a protection against Bad Faith, no further consideration of Sanctions is needed. Given Good Faith, the way to Peace is easy.

But how can we establish Good Faith? How can we disestablish Patriotism, or persuade Patriots to trust each other?

2

The answer lies in the fact that Patriotism is an orthodox religion, and that all orthodox religions have uneasy disciples. Patriotism exercises a moral compulsion on most people, much as Respectability compels the middle classes, or Fashion the fashionable. No woman ever loved lace curtains for their own sake ; no woman, of herself, ever wanted to force her body into 18-inch corsets, or wear a hat over one eye, or hobble herself in tight skirts. But ' the thing to do ' very easily becomes the thing which is done. The average man is as sensitive to the charge of being unpatriotic as the average woman is to the charge of being out of the fashion, and his Patriotism is as surely ordered for him as the new mode is ordered for her. Left to himself, he would be happy with his own private hopes and fears, loves and hates ; and whatever pride of country he kept in his heart would either need no public expression, or, if revealed, would not be expressed in aeroplanes.

But he is not left to himself. He is, by religion, a Patriot, and his religion demands from him subjection to the religious authorities. Whether he approves of war in the abstract, or condemns it : whether he thinks a particular war justified or unjustified : as soon as war is declared, he ceases to be a free man. Even the official exponent of Christianity subdues regretfully his Christianity to his Patriotism.

Regretfully. . . . Uneasily. . . . Those are the words which make the establishment of Good Faith possible. For Bad Faith is only to be feared under the *compulsion* of Patriotism.

Now if our leaders renounce war, then, by that renunciation, they have disestablished Patriotism :

which I have defined as 'a passionate interest in the military strength of one's country'; for one cannot take a passionate interest in something which is not there. That is to say, the compulsion of Patriotism will no longer operate on the average man. He will be free to find some other outlet for his love-of-country and pride-of-country. What outlet will he find? Is it not probable that he will now take a passionate interest in the *honour* of his country, an interest which will express itself in a determination that his country shall keep faith?

Consider the case of the average man who is neither Pacifist nor Public Patriot: the man who wants to be left in peace, but fears to do anything for peace lest he should be thought unpatriotic. He believes with all his heart that aggressive war is wrong; but obviously (he says) if you are attacked, you must defend yourself. He will pledge himself not to support his country in a war of aggression; but, when war comes, he will either accept the assurance that it is not a war of aggression, or (if he finds this impossible) tell himself patriotically that his country's need absolves him of his pledge. He will fight, though with an uneasy conscience.

But now let his leaders, the high priests of Patriotism, *ask* him to take the pledge never to fight again in any circumstances; now let them implore him to make the pledge as binding as his conscience can make it ; now let them assure him that the honour of his country insists that he shall be true to his pledge ; now let them tell him that the only pride-of-country which his religion demands is pride in her good faith ; and what happens ? Gladly will he give the pledge, and faithfully will he keep it. For he is a free man again.

3

To resume, then, our imaginary Peace Conference.

The delegates have agreed that Universal Peace is necessary. They have agreed upon the conditions on which each country is to pledge herself to Peace. They have accepted each other's conditions. How are they to ensure Good Faith ?

I make the following crude suggestions, leaving the refinement of them to a subsequent section.

1. The oath to be taken shall be an oath to renounce aggressive *and defensive* war, and to submit *all* disputes to arbitration.

2. The oath shall be taken, in the first place, by the Leaders of each country.

3. The oath taken shall be the most solemn oath conceivable, and shall be made as publicly as possible.

4. Having themselves taken the oath, the

Leaders of each country shall instruct their people to take, individually, a similar oath. A special day shall be set apart for this: as it might be Armistice Day. For those who profess any religion the oath shall be a religious oath.

5. The Head of each religious faith which has followers in the countries concerned shall proclaim that any member of the Faith who breaks his oath —in whatever circumstances, and under whatever compulsion of Patriotism—is *ipso facto* excommunicated.

6. It shall be made clear to all concerned, both by the Leaders of the Church and the Leaders of the State, that no person is released from his oath by reason of some other person's default.

4

The Patriot will dismiss this scornfully as childish and absurd. If he will read Chapter I again, he will be reminded of the extreme childishness of war. He may also be reminded of his own childhood, when childish behaviour was corrected by the childish remedy of 'standing in the corner'. For many years Daylight Saving was scorned as childish and absurd; as, indeed, it is, since it is no more than an official recognition of the childish game of make-believe. But it was the childish game of war which established Daylight Saving.

Now I admit that this suggestion for a solemn pledge of renunciation is not only childish but unworthy of consideration, if it is not preceded by a passionate desire for Peace. The Pacifist is continually up against this difficulty: that he neither knows who he is trying to convince, nor of what he is trying to convince him. At one moment the Militarist is saying that of course he wants Peace just as much as the Pacifist, but ' human nature being what it is ' . . . and at the next, when a suggestion for dealing with human nature is made, he adds that of course one mustn't forget that ' the greatest qualities of man come out in armed conflict '. Well, all that one can do is to try to deal with each argument in turn. But the premiss of each new argument must be the conclusion of the last one. In suggesting a method by which Europe can find Peace if she wants it, I am taking it for granted, and inevitably taking it for granted, that her desire for Peace is as ardent as my own.

Now let us consider this method.

1. The oath renounces not only attack, but defence. Unless defence is also renounced, the oath is worthless. If a man pledges himself to complete abstinence from anything, he knows when he is breaking his pledge. If he pledges himself to conditional abstinence, he is leaving himself to his own interpretation of the conditions,

and his pledge has no absolute value. A renunciation of both aggressive and defensive war leaves the renouncer with the opportunity of breaking his word, but with no hope of evading it.

2. In the case of England, it would probably be enough if the King were to take the oath, for no Leader of public opinion would dare to suggest that the King be forsworn. In countries under a Dictatorship, the oath would be taken both by the Dictator and the titular Head (if any); and in democratic countries by the Leaders of the different parties.

3. The nature of the oath should be suited to the nature of the oath-taker. To some men an oath taken on the Bible is sacred; to others an oath over the tomb of the Unknown Warrior, or beneath the national flag. Those who were not afraid of the sacrifice which they have demanded so constantly and so fearlessly from others, could pledge themselves to death in the event of their oath being dishonoured. It may be said that, if a Hitler were to be conceived as capable of breaking his oath to renounce war, he would be equally capable of breaking his oath to commit suicide. But it is just possible that the knowledge that an honourable Hindenburg would now be forced to commit suicide might not be without its effect. [The English Patriot may spend two minutes considering what effect such a pledge from the

PATRIOTISM AND PLEDGES

King of England would have on his martial spirit.]

4–5. It is these provisions which give us most hope of an enduring Peace. Now, for the first time in the history of the world, men will not have to divide their allegiance between Honour and Patriotism, between their Country and their God. In a previous chapter I argued that the Churches had only given their approval to State Murder because it was the traditional method of serving the State; and, in an imaginary conversation with a clergyman, I exhibited him (and, I think correctly) as resenting the suggestion that his Church would sanction State Adultery or Recantation of Faith. Well, now the traditional form of Patriotism has been renounced. If Christians are to be Patriotic still, they have first to deny Christ in a new form. They have first to break a solemn oath taken in the name of their God. Will the Churches absolve them of this too? I do not see how they can. Nor do I see how any honourable man is to be absolved by his own conscience.

6. This provision is, of course, essential. If once we can excuse our own bad faith by saying that 'the other man began it', we are back in the old morass of treacheries and fears and false accusations. We can only stand firmly on an unconditional pledge for which each one of us, alone, bears the responsibility.

5

Now before the Elder Statesman can dismiss this Peace Plan as 'absurd', he must be quite clear in his mind as to where the absurdity begins. For instance:

(i) It *is* absurd to think that, if the Great Men of Europe still see any advantage to themselves or their countries in war or the threat of war, they will make any serious attempt to renounce war.

(ii) It *is* absurd to think that, if they were to pretend to renounce war for the purpose of taking advantage of each other, their pledges would have any value.

On the other hand:

(i) It is *not* absurd to think that, if the Great Men of Europe were convinced that another war would bring disaster to Europe and to themselves, they would be determined to prevent it.

(ii) It is *not* absurd to think that, if they renounced war in order to prevent another war, their pledges would have a certain initial value.

In my Peace Plan I am allowing the Great Men of Europe a *minimum* of intelligence, a *minimum* of humanity, a *minimum* of honour. I am suggesting that they are just intelligent enough to realize that another European war will mean complete disaster for the world; just humane enough to wish to save Europe from the untellable horror of this war; just honourable enough, when they have taken a solemn oath to save Europe, to intend to keep their word.

The Elder Statesman may say that it is absurd to credit Great Men and Elder Statesmen with even this little intelligence, even this little humanity, even this little honour. He may be right. In any case I should agree with him that one must not over-stress the humanity and honour of Patriotic Politicians. For this reason I reinforce their humanity and their honour with the humanity and the honour of the Common Man, in which I am a great believer. Perhaps it is this which is absurd of me : to believe that the great majority of mankind is honourable and kindly. The Elder Statesman must tell me.

But on the (possibly absurd) assumption that Peace Conferences are trying to ensure Peace, I think that my suggestion (or, for that matter, anybody's suggestion) is worth consideration. For fifteen years Peace Conferences have been padding up and down the well-worn steps to Deadlock. Here they are :

1. War depends on armaments.
2. Therefore the way to Peace is by Disarmament.
3. But nations won't disarm until they are guaranteed Security.
4. Therefore they must have Security.

5. Which can only be given by Sanctions.
6. Which depend on armaments. (*See* 2.)

It is not surprising that, after fifteen years, this approach to Peace has left us exactly where we were. Such a method of approach could not possibly leave us anywhere else. Peace stands at her unbolted door, inviting us into her temple, and we tell ourselves, with irresistible logic and a completely French lucidity of thought, that if only we could batter our way through its impregnable walls, then we should be able to unbolt the door and let ourselves in. My great Peace Plan is merely a fanciful and childish suggestion that we should walk in through the unbolted door now. I suggest that there is no need to bother about Security or Disarmament until we have decided on Peace. When once we have pledged ourselves to Peace, then Security and Disarmament will inevitably follow.

Now let us consider the Elder Statesman's objections to this plan.

E.S. *It is fanciful, childish, absurd.*

So was the burial of the Unknown Warrior. So is the Two Minutes' Silence. What the Elder Statesman really means is that it is not the normal way in which Great Statesmen dispose of the lives of the inarticulate. Diplomatists, in fact, ' don't do these things '. They don't. Indeed in the present matter they have not done anything.

PATRIOTISM AND PLEDGES

E.S. The pledge could only be binding, at best, upon the present leaders of Europe, who might at any moment lose power.

Obviously the pledge would be renewed whenever necessary. In constitutional countries it would be incorporated in the constitution that nobody could hold office who had not taken the oath. In unconstitutional countries, when a new Dictator seized power, his Government would not be recognized until he had pledged himself to Peace. Similarly with the new generation: each of whom would take the oath on coming of age, or at some earlier date. These are details which could very easily be worked out. The important step is the first one: the revival of Honour.

E.S. Nothing is said about Disarmament.

Disarmament will look after itself. It is improbable that a nation will spend millions on something which is no longer required. Certainly in a democratic country it would be difficult to reconcile the taxpayers to such an expense. ' Vote for Baldwin and an Air Force which he is pledged not to use ' is an appeal as little conceivable as likely to be effective. Even a Dictator must try to preserve his popularity. ' More taxes for the dishonour of our great country ' will not be Mussolini's most popular slogan. On the other hand, armaments necessary for internal security, or for the protection of a country's nationals outside Europe, will be maintained as before, but without fear of evoking rivalry from any other country. They will gradually adjust themselves to a country's real needs, instead of being artificially determined by the fears and jealousies of a neighbour. Clearly the armament problem stands or falls with the pledge. The idea of administering a solemn pledge of honour with all the ceremony which I have suggested, and then setting up a commission in order to see that it is being kept, is to make the word honour entirely meaningless.

E.S. No provision is made for Security. If you pledge yourself not to defend your country, what security can you possibly have against attack?

There is no such thing as complete security in this world, and such security as there is does not necessarily depend upon the sanctions of force. The greatest safeguard which the average man has against being murdered is not the death penalty, but the fact that he has given very few people the desire to murder him, and that these few do not wish to have the sin of murder on their consciences. There is, of course, a penalty for murder. There is no penalty for ' accidentally ' jogging your neighbour's arm as he is about to drink, and upsetting his glass over his nice new clothes. Yet we shall lunch at our clubs to-morrow, reasonably safe against this form of attack, and willing to dispense with the complete security of a waterproof suit.

One might ask the Elder Statesman : What security has his country now against attack ? None. All that she can hope to obtain from the aeroplanes which she is building is security against ultimate defeat. If it is ' security ' not to be the underneath one when the world crashes, why has Europe spent all these years trying to avert the crashing of the world ? The Elder Statesman may reply that it is the enemy's knowledge that you are able to attack him which gives you security against attack. If this were so, then there would never have been a war in the history of the world.

The security which is now offered to nations is a different sort of security. It is the security of a country's honour : a moral force which has never yet been allowed expression. I suggest giving it a trial.

Up to now a country's honour has been in the hands of its politicians. Politicians have been taught to serve a tradition which separates personal honour from political honour, and regards the Safety of the State as an end which justifies any dishonourable means. This tradition has obtained a sort of uneasy acceptance, much as graft has obtained acceptance in America, or divorce-court perjury in England. But we can always disencumber ourselves of a tradition, if we really want to. A man in the divorce-court, otherwise esteemed honourable, swears before his God to tell the truth, the whole truth, and nothing but the truth ; but he has this reservation in his mind: that, traditionally, it is the duty of a man of honour to lie on behalf of a woman. Suppose, however, that he were to take the oath in this form : ' I swear before God to tell the truth, the whole truth, and nothing but the truth, pledging myself as a man of honour to renounce utterly, in His name, the tradition of perjury which hitherto has been esteemed honourable in this court '—well then he would find perjury a little more difficult. Indeed, impossible . . . until, in the course of years a new tradition of perjury had grown up.

If nations solemnly pledge themselves, in the way I have suggested, to renounce both attack and defence, there are three reasons why these pledges should have a sanctity which they have failed to earn in the past.

(i) The God within us never quite surrenders. Even the worst man is forced to make some concession to his conscience. This is why so many thieves begin by ' borrowing ' ; this is why so many murderers live in a romantic world of their own, in which their protestations of innocence can be the protestations of a genuinely wronged man, whose murders are not murders. A pledge to renounce both attack and defence gives the breaker of it no mental escape. He stands, as Mussolini has said in another connection, ' face to face with himself in the alternative of death '; death to his soul: death to himself as a man of honour. Doubtless there are dishonourable men in the world; doubtless some of them find their way into politics. But it is much easier for them to be dishonourable when they can persuade themselves that they are still being men of honour.

(ii) Not only will national leaders be unable to deceive themselves, but they will be unable to deceive their countrymen. As things are, any government can proclaim its pacific intentions towards another country: can pledge itself against aggressive action, while increasing what it calls its defensive armaments: can declare war against the other country, on the plea that she is arming herself in an aggressive manner: and then, without the slightest difficulty, can persuade its people that it is utterly innocent of offence, and that all the aggression came from the wicked enemy. Under the new pledge this will no longer be possible. If a statesman is now going to break faith, he will have to do it, not only with his eyes open, but before the open eyes of the world.

(iii) Even the most shameless sinner hopes to profit by his sin. Politicians may be prepared to break faith, but their broken faith will achieve nothing without popular support. They will find that the common man is amenable no longer to Flags, Bands, Loud Speakers and all the panoply of Patriotism. The honour of his country is now, for the first time, in the common man's keeping.

E.S. The fact remains that one faithless nation MIGHT break faith and attack another nation. This being so, it is unthinkable that nations should renounce defence.

It is only unthinkable because nobody has ever tried thinking about it. To an inhabitant of Mars (or even to a simple savage) it is ' unthinkable ' that England's honour should be bound up in the mutilation of women and children. It is unthinkable that we should still have the same thoughts about war, now that it means the murder of the defenceless, as we had when it meant hand-to-hand fighting between professional soldiers. It is unthinkable that, for the sixteen years subsequent to a war which caused the deaths of ten million men and a million women and children, we should have been busy inventing new and more horrible forms of death. It is unthinkable that, after a war which brought winner and loser alike to the verge of anarchy and ruin, which destroyed equally a generation of the conquered and a generation of the conquerors, we should still think of war in terms of victory and defeat.

Let us be clear about this. As a *new* thought modern war is completely unthinkable. Tell the

PATRIOTISM AND PLEDGES

innocent visitor from another world that two people were killed in Serajevo, and that the best that Europe could do about it was to kill eleven million more ; read to him the European Theory of War as I have put it down in Chapter VIII ; and, when he has recovered from the wave of horror or the gust of laughter which sweeps over him, he will say : ' But it is *unthinkable* that beings endowed with souls and intelligences should behave like this.' Not until you tell him that the human race is supposed to have descended from the apes, and has been descending steadily for a million years, will he be able to understand it.

So, while the visitor from Mars is trying to get into his head an entirely unthinkable ' acceptance of war ', let us, in the next chapter, try to get into our heads an entirely unthinkable ' refusal of war '. He was helped by remembering that we are descended from the apes. It is possible that we may be helped by remembering that we have aspirations towards God.

CHAPTER XVII
REFUSAL OF WAR

I

'*THE fact remains*' (*says the Elder Statesman*) '*that one faithless nation might break faith and attack another nation. This being so, it is unthinkable that a nation should renounce defence.*'

The first thing which we must try to realize is this: that the physical *possibility* of disaster is not in itself alarming. It is only alarming when it reaches a certain degree of probability. There are a few homicidal maniacs in England. If one broke out and attacked the Elder Statesman, he would be glad of a revolver with which to defend himself. He has, however, renounced the use of a revolver. Yet the fact remains that one homicidal maniac *might* break out and attack him.

To say, then, that, because one nation *might* break faith, it is unthinkable that other nations should renounce defence, is to say something which, in itself, is meaningless. It is I, of course, who have put these meaningless words into the Elder Statesman's mouth ; but I have put them there because they do represent the common habit of thought in Peace Conferences : I mean the determination of politicians to take no risk. Their philosophy seems to be that, if one risks anything, one risks everything, and is a traitor ; and that, if one is a Patriot, it is one's duty to risk nothing. Moreover, the security which they seek is always a physical security rather than a moral security.

Now if any reader considers his private life in relation to this question of risk, he will become aware

(i) that against many *possible* dangers he seeks no security whatever ;

(ii) that the security which he has sought, and apparently obtained, against other dangers, has often proved to be worthless ;

(iii) that against certain dangers moral security is of much greater value than physical security.

The first two facts are so easily recognizable as to need no illustration. As for the third, one may perhaps point out that by no compulsion of force is one's wife prevented from removing her shoes and stockings during an afternoon call at the Vicar's. But one has complete moral security against this disaster. Only a fool (or, it may be, a politician just returned from a Peace Conference) would insist on her wearing non-detachable stockings.

Now it is true that, if all the nations of Europe pledge themselves to renounce war, any one nation which was prepared to break its pledge would be able to force its will (as far as force is effective) upon another nation. But in itself that means nothing. What we have to consider is the *likelihood* of a nation breaking its pledge.

Well, shall we discuss the possibility of England forswearing herself? The King has given his word; Mr. Baldwin, that honourable man, standing in the shadow of the Cenotaph, has pledged himself by all that he holds most sacred; the Editor of the *Morning Post*, at the altar of his village church, has sworn to renounce war, and rumours of war, and incitements to war . . . and then what happens? The Editor writes a leading article demanding military action against Germany; the Cabinet decides on mobilization; the King signs an Order in Council; and all the people cheer. Is that likely? Does even the most fervid patriot want to discuss the possibility of that? We *know* that it could not happen.

Nevertheless, we are called ' Perfidious Albion '. And what Perfidious Albion is anxious about is, not her own good faith, for of that she is assured, but of the good faith of other countries ; particularly of Germany. This must seem humorous to other countries ; particularly to Germany. Let us however take it seriously, and consider seriously the possibility of Germany forswearing herself.

It is a little difficult to discuss Germany now, for the Germany of to-day may not be the Germany of to-morrow. In any case, the Germany which we are assuming to have taken the pledge is not the Germany of to-day. She is, by reason of the fact that she has taken the pledge, (i) a Germany which recognizes that another European war will be disastrous, and (ii) a contented Germany. Let me remind the reader of the *order* (for the order is what matters) in which, it is assumed, the steps to Peace have been taken.

First : Realization that Universal Peace is a vital necessity to Europe.

Second : Conditional acceptance of Peace if certain claims are satisfied.

Third : Settlement of claims.

Fourth : Complete renunciation both of aggression and defence.

Germany, a contented Germany (or, at least, an apparently contented Germany) has reached the fourth step, and has taken the pledge with all the solemnity suggested. Will she break the pledge ?

I can do no more than say that I feel quite certain that she wouldn't, and that she couldn't : that it would be as surely a moral impossibility for her to break the pledge as it would be for France or England. Indeed, I should say that the pledge would be even more likely to be binding on Germany than on France ; not because I put Germany's honour, or desire for peace, higher than France's, but because the one country is notoriously sensitive to foreign opinion, and the other country is notoriously insensitive. It may be said that in the last war Germany broke her pledge not to violate Belgium. She did ; but she was never happy until she produced ' evidence ' that France had already decided to break the pledge first. Even now the clause in the Peace Treaty which Germany resents most (and more than any which have brought material losses upon her) is the clause which puts upon her the responsibility for the war. Even now, when she seems, as never before, to have made physical force her god, she shows a continuous, and to other nations astonishing, desire to justify herself in the eyes of the world. Mussolini never cared so for the moral judgment of others ; nor, in similar circumstances, would France ; nor, even, would England. Germany, more than any other country, needs to be ' right with herself '.

REFUSAL OF WAR

Now the whole point of the pledge which I have outlined will be this : that no country can break it and remain right with herself ; no individual can break it and not know that he is forsworn. A pledge to renounce aggression only : a pledge contingent on its observance by others : a pledge in any respect conditional is completely worthless. The nations of Europe have proved its worthlessness over a hundred million dead bodies, and in the proof have made the phrase 'a country's honour' no more than a scornful jest. But let the pledge be absolute : put the national conscience face to face with itself in the alternative of death : and immediately 'a country's honour' will begin to mean something.

(*Yet the fact remains that Germany might break faith. This being so, it is unthinkable that nations should renounce defence.*)

I say that the unthinkable thing is that Germany, or any other nation, should break faith. I say that it is impossible that she should break faith. No 'sanctions', no 'security', makes the invasion of France impossible ; all that sanctions and security can do is to make invasion dangerous and expensive. The taking of this pledge, in the way I have suggested, makes the invasion of France impossible. It makes it 'impossible' in the only way in which it could be impossible : that is, morally impossible.

PEACE WITH HONOUR

I invite the Elder Statesman to rely upon his imagination rather than upon his knowledge of history. I invite him to attempt to conceive this tremendous concerted attempt by the Powers to overthrow war; to picture this solemn occasion when the Great Statesmen pledge themselves before their God, by all that they hold most sacred, to renounce for ever the use of armaments against each other: a pledge taken with none of the reservations of the past, a pledge taken, indeed, with an explicit renunciation of the traditions and patriotisms of the past, taken with an explicit recognition of its absolute nature. I invite him to imagine this solemn occasion broadcast over the world on screen and loud-speaker; I invite him to imagine (if he can) one of those who had so pledged his honour, breaking that solemn pledge, and knowing as he broke it that, on the morrow, in every cinema-theatre in every little town, on every gramophone in every little house, his dishonour would be paraded.

No knowledge of history will help the Elder Statesman to appreciate the value of such a consecration. His automatic reflex to any mention of the word 'pledge' has always been the reflection, in his best realistic manner, that pledges are made to be broken, and treaties easily torn up. Let him forget the traditional misfaith of the past, and imagine an unhistorical tradition inaugurated in an unhistorical ceremony. Just as it was necessary to bring a new mind to the contemplation of war as it is to-day, so it is necessary to bring a new mind to the contemplation of Peace as it could be to-morrow.

2

Sympathetic Reader. As I understand it, the supreme value of this pledge of yours, apart from the solemnity of it and the publicity with which it is surrounded, lies in the fact that it is an absolute pledge from which there is no possible mental escape.

M. Yes.

S.R. That is to say, if you break faith, you break faith, and it's no excuse to say that somebody else was forsworn first.

M. Yes.

S.R. And the moral force which will prevent a country from breaking her word of honour in future is the universal condemnation which would accompany such treachery? The horror of the civilized world, so to speak.

M. The moral force which prevents an honourable man from breaking his word of honour is his honour. The moral force which prevents a dishonourable man from breaking his word of honour is his desire to maintain an appearance of honour.

S.R. The point I was going to make is this. A liar might be kept from lying by the public opinion of truthful men. But he wouldn't be kept from lying by the public opinion of other liars. Now would it not be possible for one faithless country to persuade herself, in the good old way, that every other country was about to break her word, and, having persuaded herself of this, to resort to arms again? The 'horror of the civilized world' would then mean no more to her than the 'mock-horror' of countries as guilty as herself. If the faithless country were Germany, she would placate her conscience with the thought: 'We tried to establish a tradition of honour among nations, but France showed that it was impossible. It is now evident that there can never be such a thing as honour among nations, and only a hypocrite would pretend otherwise.'

M. Is Germany the only country which 'resorts to arms'?

S.R. In the first place, yes, although she would pretend to herself that France began it. I am suggesting that there is still this possibility of what you call mental escape. I agree with you that it is supremely important that there shouldn't be, but I think that there is. I think that a Hitler could persuade himself and his countrymen that Europe had pledged herself to an impossibility, and, by that fact, was released from the pledge.

The Sympathetic Reader must exercise his imagination too. No country suddenly ' resorts to arms ' just for the fun of resorting to arms. If English airmen flew over to Italy, a year after Europe's renunciation of war, and dropped bombs on Rome, they would drop them with some object. Presumably Italy would have been informed of the object; presumably some sort of dispute relative to the object would have arisen between England and Italy. By the terms of the pledge this dispute has to be submitted to arbitration. It would be impossible for a guilty England to persuade herself that she was ready to keep her oath, but that Italy refused arbitration. Italy has only to announce her consent to arbitration in accordance with her pledge, and her honour is secure. If English airmen then dropped bombs on Rome, it is difficult to see what remnant of honour, even among themselves, English statesmen would manage to preserve. But, of course, such a resort to arms is inconceivable.

However, let us discuss the inconceivable. Or rather, let us discuss something which does not seem so inconceivable to the Patriot: the possibility that Germany, still armed (or secretly re-armed), breaks her pledge, and demands something from a defenceless England. Then what?

Then, presumably, if she wants it as urgently as that, she gets it. I say ' as urgently as that ', for now there is no escape from public dishonour, no escape from public contempt. No excuse to herself or to the rest of the world is now available. Here is a treachery so black that in its presence the violation of Belgian neutrality becomes an offence as harmless as the whitest of lies. It is probable, then, that if her need is so urgent, it would have been satisfied at the Peace Conference, when (it will be remembered) all urgent needs were satisfied in the endeavour to obtain peace. If it is a need which has since arisen, it is possible that England would now be prepared to satisfy it.

If not——

Then presumably Germany takes it; as she would take it if she had declared war on, and defeated, England.

An inconceivable thought to the old-style Patriot.

But to English men and women who know that war is wrong: to English men and women who love England: to English men and women who think that the supreme virtues are moral virtues, and who are more greatly concerned with the

REFUSAL OF WAR

honour of their country than with its possessions : to many English people, not an inconceivable thought. A thought no more inconceivable, no more horrifying, than the thought that a burglar might break in and steal.

England would have lost something (and it might be something which all English people would regret losing) ; but she would not have lost her honour, for it is only the sanctity of her word which has made material loss possible ; she would not have lost her pride, for the ' defeat ' which she has suffered is a defeat which she has deliberately risked for the salvation of the world.

I should be proud to think that England would take this risk. I should be proud to think of England risking something for a cause outside herself. Whether we are Patriots, or just plain men and women who love our country, we want to be proud of England. How can pride-of-country be an admirable quality, an inspiring quality, if it is nothing more than a pride of material possession ? It is difficult for a man to be proud of his name, if, through the centuries, his family has shown no attribute more noble, more selfless, than a determination to keep trespassers off its property. The Great Powers, which have inspired through the centuries so much patriotism, have offered their devotees no greater inspiration than this; they have proclaimed no higher ideal than the ideal of self-advancement and self-protection. The willingness of a Great Power to fight about anything or nothing: the willingness of its Great Statesmen to sacrifice to their national ambitions the lives of others: these have been exhibited so lavishly and so continuously that now, surely, they may be taken for granted. If these be virtues, nobody will deny them to England. Were England now to seek a new virtue: were she to take the risk of sacrifice in the cause of Peace and for the saving of the world; then, for every vocal Patriot who cried out, a thousand quiet English men and women would feel in their hearts a pride too deep for words.

3

So I shall re-write the paragraph at the head of the chapter in this way:

Granted the premiss, *it is unthinkable that one faithless nation should break faith, and attack another nation. Even if this were not so, nations should take the risk of it, for a cause higher than any national cause, the cause of humanity.*

The premiss is that Europe wants Peace.

It is certain that the people of Europe want Peace. They have never wanted anything else.

The premiss, then, is that the Dictators of Europe want Peace.

As I said in Chapter XV, the Peace of Europe is in their hands.

CHAPTER XVIII

'WOMEN AND CHILDREN FIRST'

ONCE more, then, I address the Great Men of Europe as if they were men of my acquaintance : men, that is, not without intelligence, not without humanity, not without honour.

Gentlemen, the Peace of Europe is in your hands.

One of you has said that he renounces the idea of Perpetual Peace, for the reason that War stamps the mark of nobility upon nations. Yet I doubt whether another war will stamp the mark of nobility upon the Italian nation any more clearly than did the last war; any more clearly than the current war is stamping the mark of nobility upon Bolivia and Paraguay. In England we have a saying *Noblesse oblige*, by which we mean that nobility has obligations. The nobility which the next war is to confer will compel you to sacrifice to your creed the lives of thousands of women and children. In England we have another saying : ' Women and children first ', by

'WOMEN AND CHILDREN FIRST'

which we mean that they shall be the first to be saved. Beneath the crest of your new-found nobility you also will write ' Women and children first ', meaning by this that they shall be the first to be sacrificed.

I ask you to think about this. In the old wars your men fought with men, and tried to kill them, and in fighting took the risk of being killed. In the next war your women will be exposed to a death against which no defence is possible ; and your men will be forced not to fight with, but to kill, in every circumstance of horror, defenceless women and children. Do you think that this is going to stamp the mark of nobility upon you or your people ? Even in the most romantic film-story (such as, if you will forgive me for saying so, you seem at times to be living) the American hero in his beleaguered shack is wont to surrender himself rather than expose the heroine to the danger of a stray shot. Is it too much to ask of a Roman hero that he should surrender his ambitions in order to avoid exposing Italian women to mutilation and death ?

Once more I beg you all to tear away the veil of sentimental mysticism through which you have looked at war, and try to see it as it really is. The words which you have associated with it for so many years : ' victory ', ' defeat ', ' indemnities ', ' non-combatants ' ; these words have now lost their meaning; just as the word war has lost its meaning. It is no longer war. It is something for which the word has not yet been invented, something as far removed from the Napoleonic Wars as they were from a boxing-match. This new thing which you are asked to renounce is a degradation which would soil the beasts, a lunacy which would shame the madhouse. In renouncing it, you will be renouncing nothing which History has accepted or Poetry idealized, nothing in which your countries have found profit or your countrymen glory.

You and your like have spent fifteen years in the official pursuit of Peace, and you have not advanced one step nearer to your goal. Indeed, some think that your pursuit of Peace has only brought us nearer to War; that all this talk of Security has raised in the nations of Europe a new feeling of insecurity, and that discussion of Disarmament has merely provided new matter for disagreement. Again, then, I urge you to decide now whether you want Peace. If your aim is (as sometimes it seems to be) to combine the maintenance of the idea of War with the maintenance of a condition of Peace, then there is no hope for us but this : that in the condition of War which you will surely establish we may be able to maintain the idea of Peace, so that, when you are dead and dishonoured, what is left of the world may

'WOMEN AND CHILDREN FIRST'

try again. It is not much to hope for, but it is all that you have allowed us.

If you want Peace, you must renounce the *idea* of War. If you do this, then the way to Peace is easy, and the vast majority of your people will follow you along it with thankfulness.

It has been said with authority that 'the next war will mean the end of civilization'. It has been said with authority that the 'combatants' in the next war 'will include not only the manhood but the women and children of each nation'. Is it not more important to discuss the truth or untruth of these statements than to discuss the security or the insecurity of France? If they are true, then to discuss the 'security' of France in terms of armaments is only to waste time which may be vital, for the security of the world rests upon a renunciation of the use of armaments.

Let me give you one more proof of this.

By this morning's post I have received a circular from a newly formed body which calls itself the '*Hands off Britain* Air Defence League'. It cries in large letters:

WHY WAIT FOR A BOMBER TO LEAVE BERLIN AT 4 O'CLOCK AND WIPE OUT LONDON AT 8?

And then, in the Patriot's best *Boy's Own Paper* manner:

CREATE A NEW WINGED ARMY OF LONG-RANGE

PEACE WITH HONOUR

BRITISH BOMBERS TO SMASH THE FOREIGN HORNETS IN THEIR NESTS.

Well, other countries have their Patriots too. Doubtless there is a *Hands off Germany* Air Defence League, a *Hands off France* Air Defence League, a *Hands off Italy* Air Defence League. Doubtless all these Leagues are crying : ' Why wait for a bomber to leave London (Rome, Paris) at 4 o'clock and wipe out Berlin (Paris, Rome) at ——' the appropriate hour. Doubtless they are all urging their fellow-patriots to create a new winged army of long-range German (French, Italian) bombers to smash the foreign hornets in their nests. That is the state to which you have brought Europe in your search for peace : this is the security which you offer us.

Now why, when nobody is putting his hands on Britain, does anybody cry ' Hands off Britain ' ? Why, when we have no serious cause of quarrel with any foreign country, are Englishmen invited to ' smash the foreign hornets in their nests ' ? The answer is that to the New War there is no defence but attack, and that the attack must precede the attack of the enemy. If London is not to be ' wiped out ' at 8 by bombers leaving Berlin at 4, then Berlin must be ' wiped out ' at 3 by bombers leaving London at 11. And the only German defence to the bombers leaving London at 11 is for the bombers leaving Berlin at 6 to

'WOMEN AND CHILDREN FIRST'

'wipe them out' at 10. . . . And so on for ever. Is it, then, surprising that every Patriot is in a panic lest some foreign Patriot should begin first? Is it not inevitable that, when the New War comes, it will come for no other reason than that nations were afraid of its coming; that, so far from being 'a war to end war', it will be a war to end the terrifying uncertainty of peace?

There is one way, and only one way, to arrest this war, and that is to renounce war. I have suggested a method by which this renunciation might be made a reality. You will call it 'impossible'. When we call a thing impossible we mean that it has never happened in our experience. A renunciation of war has never happened in our experience, and therefore any method of effecting it is 'impossible'; until we have tried it.

I have assumed, perhaps too hopefully, your intelligence, your humanity, your honour. I wish I could believe in your imagination. I am afraid that the 'realism' upon which France so prides herself has conquered you. You are all realists now; which means that you live in a world which does not exist: a world in which the imagination is not exercised: a world in which nothing can happen to-morrow which did not happen yesterday. Yet there are just two facts about the next war, drawn from your experience of the past and your knowledge of the present, which you should be able to get into your realistic minds:

1. If the economic life of the world barely survived a war which it entered in a condition of health, it cannot, starting in its present condition of ill-health, survive another war.

2. The next war will be a war from the air in which every woman and child will be involved. There is no defence for these women and children but an attack which will involve the enemy's women and children.

I beg you, then, to begin your next Conference by convincing yourselves, and admitting to each other your conviction, of these two facts.

I ask you next to display *all* your humanity, and decide that there shall be no such war; to exert *all* your intelligence, and realize that the only way of avoiding war is to renounce war; and to pledge *all* your honour in an oath of renunciation.

Finally, I ask you to have the grace to remember, and to remember with shame, that, through all the butchery of this next war, the lives most carefully preserved will be your own; that before the safety of any woman, before the safety of any child, will be put the safety of Mr. Ramsay MacDonald, of M. Doumergue, of Herr Hitler and of Signor Mussolini.